Did You Notice?

Did You Notice?

The Wristwatch, Upside Down Gun, Power Pole and Tire Tracks in Western Film Stills

DON CREACY

McFarland & Company, Inc., Publishers
Jefferson, North Carolina

LIBRARY OF CONGRESS CATALOGUING-IN-PUBLICATION DATA

Creacy, Don, 1930–
Did you notice? : the wristwatch, upside down gun, power pole
and tire tracks in western film stills / Don Creacy.
    p.   cm.
Includes index.

ISBN 978-0-7864-7435-6
(softcover : acid free paper) ∞

1. Western films—United States—Miscellanea.   I. Title.
PN1995.9.W4C74 2014   791.43'65878—dc23   2013051365

BRITISH LIBRARY CATALOGUING DATA ARE AVAILABLE

© 2014 Don Creacy. All rights reserved

*No part of this book may be reproduced or transmitted in any form
or by any means, electronic or mechanical, including photocopying
or recording, or by any information storage and retrieval system,
without permission in writing from the publisher.*

Front cover images © iStock/Thinkstock

Manufactured in the United States of America

*McFarland & Company, Inc., Publishers
Box 611, Jefferson, North Carolina 28640
www.mcfarlandpub.com*

Table of Contents

Acknowledgments
vi

Preface
1

Introduction
3

The Western Film Stills
7

Index
205

Acknowledgments

Getting material together for a book can require help and assistance from several people. In this case I was lucky as several people helped me find and acquire the pictures that are in this publication. I am sorry that it took me some time to finish this project because some of the people who helped me are no longer with us.

Finding pictures with something unusual in them was a chore at times. I was able to find pictures through dealers and also at film conventions. Not very many people were looking for the type of picture that I was interested in. At one film convention a dealer kept pushing pictures of Roy Rogers and Gene Autry at me. When I chose a picture of a cowboy who was right-handed but in the picture he was wearing his gun on the left side, the dealer's reaction was "That's no good!" I told him if the picture was no good, then he should lower the price or give it to me. He shut up after that. I then told him he did not listen to his customer when I told him what I was looking for.

By and large the dealers were a great help. When I explained what I was looking for they would start going through their files when they had no other customers and they came up with several photos that are in the book. Unfortunately, in some cases these were one-time meetings and I don't recall their names. The following dealers helped me several times and I would like to say thanks for their help: Dan Schwartz, Stephen Sally, Eddie Brandt and Blackie Seymour. And a big thanks to Kathy Ceppi for her work on the computer.

Preface

At one time in the United States, the highlight of the week for youngsters (and adults) was going to the movies to see their cowboy heroes. This happened from the silent days of movies to the mid–1950s. Then television — and the old movie theaters started losing ground.

During this time the movie theaters would have on display scenes from movies that would soon be shown at that theater as well as scenes from the movie now showing. These pictures would come in different sizes with different names; one sheet, half sheet, lobby cards, black and white stills, etc. These pictures would be in display cases to entice the patrons to come back to see another movie. Sometimes the theater would display lobby cards which were in color, causing some concern for the juvenile clientele who were used to seeing their Saturday heroes in black and white on the screen.

For movie fans all over the world I want to emphasize that this book is not making fun of or putting down the western films that we grew up with. Although most of these images contain mistakes, oversights, and bad judgment, these flaws do not detract from the films and in many cases appear only in the stills.

As a kid I can remember coming out of the theater and stopping in the lobby to look at the pictures on display of the movie I had just seen. At that age I noticed that some of the scenes on display were not actually in the movie, but this did not detract from my enjoying the movie.

This book is dedicated to people all over the world that remember going to the movies, silent or sound, color or black and white, and enjoying the thrills and laughs as they watched the screen in theaters ranging from a glorious palace to the grubby little place down by the railroad tracks. For some, valuable lessons were learned while watching the movies such as honesty, courtesy, speaking the truth and not giving up when hard times came along, keep trying and do your best. So sit back, relax and see what you may have missed when you watched that old movie of long ago.

I have done my best to identify the people shown in the photographs, and I apologize for any mistakes. Readers are invited to send corrections or additional information to me in care of the publisher.

Some of these pictures appeared earlier in a series published in *Classic Images*.

Thanks to numerous people that helped with locating pictures and a special thanks to my wife Rosalind for putting up with my third childhood.

Introduction

In the movie business, publicity has always been essential. Even before television and long before the Internet, movies had competition from newspapers, radio, books and all kinds of magazines. Making money on a movie meant promoting it.

In this book we are dealing with movie stills that were used in advertising a movie. In the early days of movies, a lot of advertising was just words, not pictures. You may wonder how non–English reading people would know what the movie was about. When I was quite young, I asked my mother if she had ever gone to a silent movie. I was informed that silent movies were all they had when she started going to the movies. She said that people of one nationality would gather together. One area of the theater had people that spoke German; another area had people with a Slavic dialect; and there were a couple of small groups speaking other languages. A lot of these people could speak English but could not read English.

Later on, the theater would have an ad advertising the movie on the front of the theater and in the newspaper. There would be a picture of a cowboy if the movie was a western; a man and woman in formal dress was the clue for a society drama; and a man creeping up on the good-looking hero meant a mystery movie.

Initially these pictures were all black-and-white; color came later. Sometimes the poster would be a full sheet and sometimes a half sheet. The half sheet poster would fill up half of the display case. Then the bottom half would have lobby cards or stills. Both were the work of the still photographer. The lobby cards would be in color. Some display cases would have only still pictures. It was not unusual to see people stopping at several display cases to see what movies were coming.

Most studios employed publicists and still photographers whose job was to promote the movie. Still photographers had a hectic time if they were working on a film that had a lot of action in it. They could not ask that a scene be done over so they could get a picture. Not only did they need to get a shot during an action scene but they had to be diplomatic and get players to pose for a short time at the end of a take. And we should remember that some of the people that we saw on screen were not nice people off-camera. Another chore of the still man: taking a photograph of each set in case they had to do some retakes and had to duplicate the set.

In a conversation with Bud Thackery, cameraman at Republic Studios, he talked about the difference between the cameraman and the still photographer. Bud informed

Introduction

me very quickly that he was never a still photographer. The cameraman had more responsibility and had input into the filming of a scene while the still photographer had nothing to do with the filming of a scene.

Most studios hired one or more still photographers. They would need a still man for each movie being filmed at a given time. This would not be true of the small independent producers that filmed one picture at a time, often finishing in five days. The still man would not work very long on these movies.

If there were scenes of a large number of Indians attacking a wagon train or a stampede of cattle or buffalo, anything with a large number of people or animals, the "B" studio and the independent film producer would buy film of these scenes to use in other movies. This was called stock footage. The stock footage would sometimes be quite old and you could tell the difference when it came on the screen. The cameraman and the still photographer would film and take pictures of the hero as he rides along waving his hat at five or six cows, trying to stop the stampede. Sometimes you would see this scene in a movie two or three times. These scenes would be inserted into the stampede scene and the still pictures would be on display at the movie theater.

The collecting of the pictures in this book was not planned, it just happened. While visiting a friend in Ohio, I visited a small town which was almost all antique stores. In one store I decided there was nothing there that I was interested in and told my wife I would be waiting in a chair that looked like it would not collapse. On a table next to the chair I found a magazine to look through. Under the magazine were four stills from a movie that Tex Fletcher made for Grand National (B-minus all the way) called *Six Gun Rhythm* (1939). There was one still that I thought was ... *different*. I asked the dealer about it. He said I could have all four for fifty cents. I was only interested in the one picture but I could see he wanted to get rid of all four pictures so I made my big purchase for the day. That was the start of the collection that led to this book.

Over the years I would come across a photo that I thought would fit with what I had collected earlier. The prices have gone up a lot since I started with a 12 cent still, but what has not gone up?

Acquiring a movie still was a little difficult at one time. All advertisements including stills were to be sent to the next theater when a movie had finished its run at the theater where it had been showing. There were theater owners, managers and other workers at theaters that would latch on to a still of one of their favorite films or performers. When the manager got a call about the missing pictures, the manager would swear he sent all the material on to the next theater and blame the missing material on the theater that sent the material to him.

When TV came along, a number of the older movies would show up for viewing. TV stations would advertise a movie with a still from the movie. After a while, the stills were not used. Movie stills and other advertisements became collector's items. Today they can bring big prices.

Not all of the stills in this book have mistakes in them. Some pictures have some-

Introduction

thing missing or something that should not be there. Some pictures have newcomers who later made it to the top and also some that had been on top but were now on the way down.

Some clues in a picture are in the background. Objects can be seen that were not around in the time frame of the movie. Also people that are not in the movie can be seen. Some pictures have automobiles in them even though the movie takes place in the 1880s.

Action pictures sometimes had something in the picture that should not be there. The still photographer had a hard time centering his subject and could overlook something in the background that should not be seen. He would also ride in the camera car with other people, elbow his way to the back of the car, center his subject and take his picture and hold on to something so he would not fall out of the car.

Pictures of people (stars, villains, supporting players, extras) with their eyes closed were not unusual. Blinking one's eyes is very common; ask any politician. But ideally you don't use that kind of photo when advertising a movie or asking for a vote.

Expressions on faces in scenes with several people can be interesting. No two alike. What is serious for one person can be humorous for another.

I hope you enjoy the book.

THE WESTERN FILM STILLS

Did You Notice?

Buster Crabbe is not taking any crrhances as he has his rope and six-gun on Patti McCarthy in *Rustlers Hideout* (PRC, 1944). Buster must be afraid that if Patti gets away, she will run down to one of the cars on the far left of the picture and drive away. This shot was taken at Corriganville. The clue is the rock formation in the background where, eons ago, forces underground rearranged the surface in this area, leaving the sloping rock formations. The road behind Buster on the hillside was made for a movie dealing with Burma during World War II and it was named the Burma Road. The flat area where the cars are parked was used for chase scenes until a fort was built there for the movie *Fort Apache* (RKO, 1948).

An action scene from *Hell's Valley* (National Players/Big 4, 1931) with Wally Wales in the center dishing out the punishment. Franklyn Farnum on the right is trying to restrain Wally. Yakima Canut on the left is on the receiving end from Wally. This looks like a staged photo. There are several other people in the background involved in a brawl. Yak looks like he thinks this is a comedy, but he gets the prize in this photo; the *eyes* have it.

A scene from *Range Feud* (Columbia, 1931) with (left to right) Susan Fleming, John Wayne, Buck Jones and William Waling. Buck was the star of the movie and Wayne had a minor supporting part as the rancher's son. The B cowboy actors seldom smoked but there are some examples of smoking by the heroes in publicity shots. Note the cigarette in Buck's left hand, and his horseshoe shirt. When VCR tapes became popular, there was a tape of *Range Feud* with a picture of John Wayne on the box, but nothing about Buck Jones on the cover.

Looks like the good guys are ganging up on one of the undesirable elements. This picture is from *Colt Comrades* (UA, 1943) with (left to right) William Boyd as Hopalong Cassidy, Robert Mitchum, Andy Clyde and Jay Kirby. Yes, this is the same Robert Mitchum who later went on to much bigger pictures. This was one of several pictures that Mitchum made with Hoppy.

Looks like this encounter is taking place in the saloon (where else?). The table behind Hoppy and Mitchum is round and you can see poker chips on the top. The guy behind Hoppy's right shoulder seems to think this is funny. The guy in the background by the stairs is leaving. Maybe he figures there is going to be a brawl and this is a good time to get out of the way.

The Western Film Stills

In these photos we see Bill Elliott involved in something that the hero did not do in the B Western: Bill seems to be relaxed and enjoying himself. The first photo is from the Allied Artists movie *The Maverick* (1952) with Phyllis Coates in the foreground and Myron Healey as the sergeant (three stripes on sleeve) in the background. The four men seated on the ground are either real buddy-buddy or their feet are tied together.

In this series of movies, Bill played the role of the reformed badman or a man with faults, not the part he played in his Red Ryder pictures. Elliott admired William S. Hart, who was known for his reformed badman films. This may explain the thing we are looking for, the pipe in Bill's hand. This was a no-no for the hero in the usual B western. It also looks like Bill is wearing his cowboy boots and not military boots.

The second picture is from the movie *Waco* (Monogram, 1952), and what do we see? Bill's holding his favorite pipe while conversing with Pamela Blake and his deputy (John Hart). So now we know the pipe was not an accident.

Johnny Mack Brown (left) in *Frontier Feud* (Monogram, 1945). The ranch house behind them was lost in the 1962 fire at Monogram–Melody Ranch. Jack Ingram on the right is one dressed-up bad man. Wonder why the vest material never matched the pants? Probably cost. They would need to rent a suit instead of an oddball vest. Jack's sleeves are a little long. Note the hitch rack behind Johnny with the piece of metal anchored to the vertical post and then bent around the round hitching rail and secured on the back side. The metal part saved a lot of repair work. If there were horses tied to the hitching rack and someone fired a gun, some of the horses might rear up and try to get free and take the round rack with them. I saw that once in a movie. Don't know if it was planned or if it was an accident.

Notice the mailbox that Johnny is leaning on. The mailbox was not seen in front of the frontier ranch house until the early years of the 20th century when Rural Free Delivery became widespread. Before that, ranchers had to ride into town to get their mail. The time period for this movie was around 1890. The girl is Christine McIntyre. Did women really wear skirts that dragged on the ground at that time?

Buck Jones has just landed a right cross on villain Fred Kohler in *Outlawed Guns* (Universal, 1935). This looks like a staged photo. Kohler was very good at his trade — whether it was fighting, riding, or shooting, you name it and he did it. One of his strong points was the look he gave people which seemed to say what he expected of you: "Git!" Look at Fred's right hand. Parts of three fingers are missing, yet he could draw a gun, ride a horse, fight in the saloon, no problem. I have read several accounts about his hand: that it was deformed at birth, that he lost the fingers in a real shootout, that he had an accident while making a movie and that he lost parts of the fingers while working with dynamite. However it happened, it did not keep him from doing his job.

This scene is from *Trail Riders* (Monogram, 1942), a Range Busters film. Four outlaws have just robbed the bank and are now shooting it out with the law-abiding people of Gila Springs. Young moviegoers of this time would see some of these "bad guys" week after week but would see their favorite hero every other month. So a lot of the younger generation would recognize the villains by sight and sometimes by name.

Although these men have their faces partly covered, it's not difficult to identify them. On the right is Kermit Maynard who had his own series of films from 1935 to '37 and then played supporting parts for years. Next is Frank Ellis, who has been wounded. Frank played secondary parts from silent days to the beginning of TV. The guy with saddle bags and sleepy eyes is Tex Palmer. Of the 24 Range Busters films, Tex was in ten of them. On the left is Bud Osborne, whose career was similar to Frank Ellis's except sometimes Bud would win a part in a movie because he was one of the best at driving a stagecoach.

Notice that all four bank robbers are wearing coats. Would the coats keep them from being identified? The wardrobe person could have bought the coats for a dollar at a second-hand store or the bank robbers could have gotten an extra dollar for furnishing their own coat.

A photo from *Trails of Adventure* (American, 1935) with Buffalo Bill Jr., who is in the center, ready to give the dude in the black hat what he's asking for. The sheriff is trying to keep the peace while the comic relief is playing it safe. (All the other actors are unidentified.)

The lady on the left wears an Indian head band but the rest of her costume does not seem to fit the part of an Indian woman. The man on the porch on the left ... where did he get that necktie? Was that the style in 1935? The other thing that I noticed is above Buffalo Bill Jr.'s hat. This is a sign that you would see when a store had a telephone that the public could use. That symbol is what Bell Telephone used to advertise the availability of their product. This movie was directed by Jay Wilsey — who was also known as Buffalo Bill Jr.

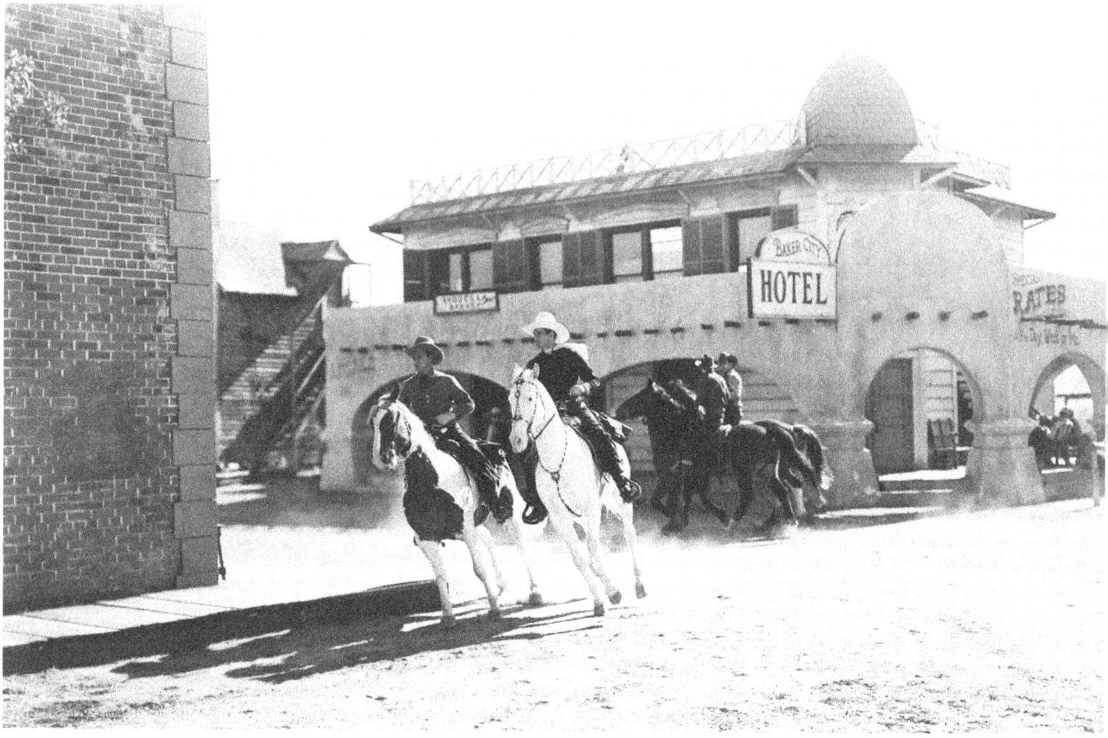
BAKER CITY
HOTEL
RATES

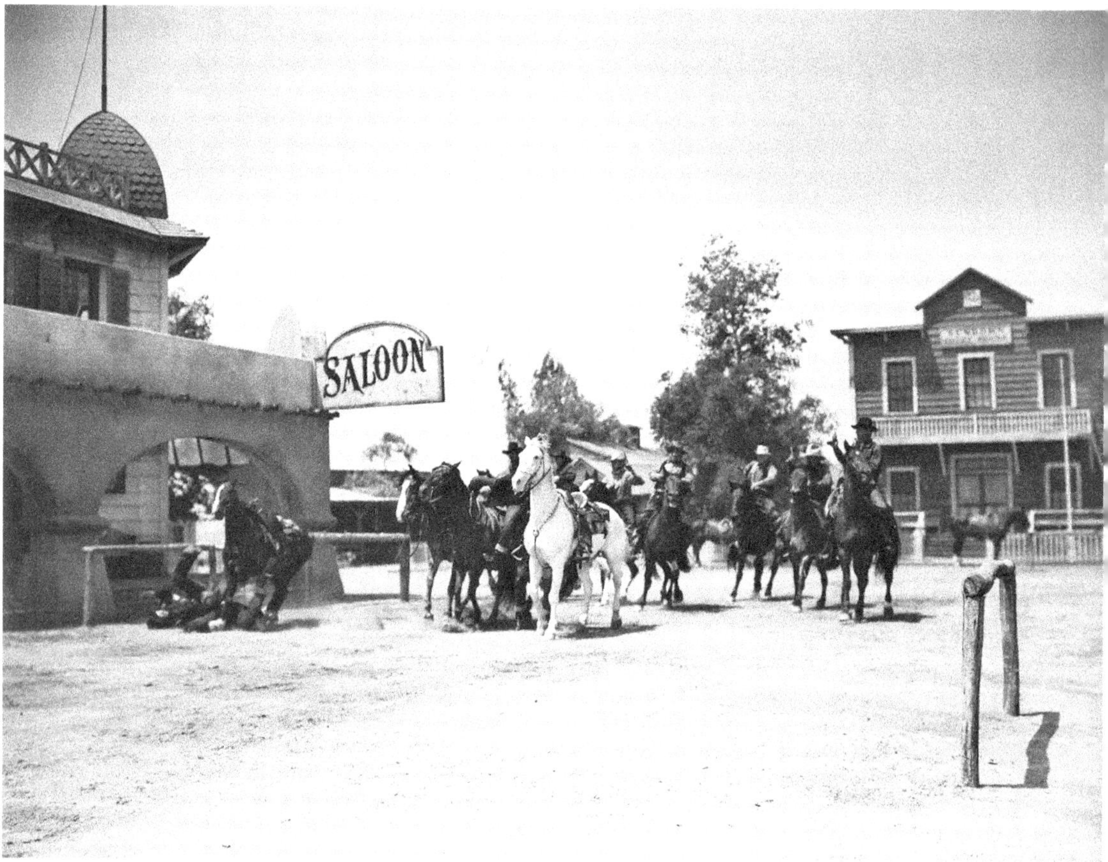
SALOON

The Western Film Stills

These two shots from unidentified movies were taken at the Columbia Ranch in Burbank, California. In one photo, Charles Starrett and Bob Nolan are riding around the corner across the street from the Baker City Hotel. In the second picture, Starrett has just pulled two people off of their horses in front of the Sundown Saloon.

Everyone can see that the hotel and saloon are the same building. It didn't take much to change from one to the other; merely switch the sign on the corner and the doors going into the building. The saloon would have bat wing swinging doors and the hotel would have full doors with glass panels.

The stucco part going around the hotel was added after several years to try and change the appearance of the western street. A few years later, the stucco part was taken down and a full two-story porch with a roof on two sides was another change, but the part on top of the roof was always a giveaway.

In these two shots, Bob Baker (or his double) is doing the jumping. Above, Bob is jumping into a wagon with a load of hay. The hay is not very high so there could be a mattress under the hay. This scene is from *Honor of the West* (Universal, 1939). Bob had to wear a hairpiece in front as there was not much hair in that area. It's a little surprising to see him or his double without his hat on.

In the second picture, *with* his hat on, Bob or the stunt man is about to jump onto someone who looks like Jack Kirk. This photo would get the kids to come and see the movie and this scene might not be in the movie. This picture is taken from a low angle, so the distance looks greater than it is, but I would not want to be the jumper or receiver of the jump. The guy is standing on solid ground and there's no mattress in sight.

From an unknown film.

The Western Film Stills

The Western Film Stills

Elsewhere in this book, we have pictures from movies that were set around the turn of the century, but in the background were cars from the time period that the movies were filmed. The cars in the background were a mistake. This time, let's reverse the process. In the top picture we have Kermit Maynard (center) being restrained by Jack Ingram on the right and another badman (actor unidentified) on the left. Behind this trio is a car that was part of the story. This picture is from *Valley of Terror* (Ambassador, 1937). How come the guy on the left has one pant leg inside the boot and one on the outside?

The lower photo shows Tom Tyler coming to the aid of Jeanne Martel and Marjorie Beebe in the movie *Lost Ranch* (Victory 1937). Behind them is an automobile that fit into the story. Both of these films were made for the time period they were filmed in, but did cowboys go around wearing guns on their hips in 1937? Maybe the filmmakers thought the kids would not care or notice, and maybe using the producer's car was cheaper than hiring more horses and people. A few years down the road, Autry and Rogers did this type of movie several times.

Wild Bill ELLIOTT

ZANE GREY'S "ROLL ALONG COWBOY" with Smith Ballew, Cecilia Parker, Stanley Fields

The Western Film Stills

The movie *Roll Along, Cowboy* (Principal/20th Century–Fox, 1937) starred Smith Ballew, who was a singer and band leader before going into the movies. His starring career lasted for five movies. He kept his band and singing going after his acting days. In the first picture Smith is being restrained by an unidentified player, Bud Osborne and Gordon Elliott (with six-gun). Looks like Elliott has everything under control.

In the second picture, Smith has turned the tables and laid one on Elliott. Note in the lower left hand corner it says Wild Bill Elliott.

Let's back up a bit. Gordon Elliott had been around for several years playing all kinds of parts, a lot of them at Warner Brothers Studios. A year after this movie, Elliott had the lead in the Columbia serial *The Great Adventures of Wild Bill Hickok* (1938) and the moniker of Wild Bill stuck with him through his movies at Columbia and Republic. When this movie was first released, there was nothing about Wild Bill Elliott in the advertisements. After Elliott became one of the more popular western stars, then someone decided to try and cash in on his name. The name Wild Bill Elliott was added to the advertisements when *Roll Along, Cowboy* was re-released.

Both of these pictures were taken at the same place. Note the rock formation in the center background, in the first picture just above Bud Osborne's hat, in the second picture to the left of Elliott's hat.

Did You Notice?

The Western Film Stills

The B Western of long ago reinforced some of the basic values of that time, including patriotism. The Pledge of Allegiance was part of the routine every morning in the elementary schools and in the high schools at all assemblies. Today it may not be used at all or is voluntary.

People of the younger generation (post–World War II) may find it difficult to understand what is going on in this picture from the movie *Deep in the Heart of Texas* (Universal, 1942) which featured Johnny Mack Brown (directly under the flag). To his right is Jennifer Holt, Fuzzy Knight and Tex Ritter. At the time this picture was made, when you said the Pledge of Allegiance you put your right hand over your heart and said "I pledge allegiance." Then you said the next words "to the flag" and everyone would lift their right hand toward the flag with the palm up a little and the hand pointed toward the flag. One completed the pledge in this position. If a man or boy had a hat or cap on, it was removed and he usually covered his heart with it.

In this photo you will see some variations on how the arm and hand are held. The men directly behind Tex Ritter have their arms bent. If they held their arms like Tex, their hands would cover Tex's face which would have ruined the picture. The hand of the person on the far left is an example of why the pledge was changed. With the palm down, the pledge looked like what the Germans did when they gave their pledge to Adolf Hitler. Kids sometimes would do this thinking it was funny, not considering the crimes against humanity that Hitler was committing. After some debate it was decided to give the pledge with one's right hand over the heart for the complete pledge.

This film was made during World War II. Did you notice that everyone is saluting the flag except one person: On the far left, in the foreground, one man is standing with his right arm by his side. He could have held his arm like the guy on his right, low with the arm bent so his hand would not cover up one of the principal players.

Some of the people in the movies started out in small parts and worked their way up to starring parts. One such was Kirby Grant.

Opposite top: This photo is from a Three Mesquiteers film, *Red River Range* (Republic 1938). The player on the left is unidentified, the girl is Lorna Gray (later Adrian Booth), Bob McKenzie is in back, and the others are Grant, John Wayne, Ray Corrigan, Sammy McKim and Max Terhune with Elmer.

Opposite bottom: Kirby had a supporting part in *Law Men* (Monogram, 1944) with Johnny Mack Brown. Grant (right) played the boyfriend the heroine as Johnny (left) was a little mature for her.

Above: In 1945 Kirby began starring in a series at Universal. Here he is seen with Fuzzy Knight in *Lawless Breed* (1946). He became better known a few years later when he starred in the TV series *Sky King*.

This stunt is called a transfer when the rider moves from his horse to a vehicle (buckboards, wagons, stagecoaches, etc.). In the top photo we see Bob Steele's character in a scene from a Three Mesquiteers film, *Thundering Trails* (Republic 1943), as he leaps from his horse to an enclosed wagon that looks like it was used in a medicine show. This stunt was most likely done by Bob's double; with his arm in front of his face, we cannot see who it is and that's the way it was supposed to be done. Did you notice the man's stirrups? They are in an L shape so the rider would not have any trouble getting his boots out of the stirrups when he makes the transfer.

The lower photo is a scene from *Prairie Justice* (Universal, 1938) with Bob Baker. Bob's double has just about completed his transfer to the stagecoach but did you notice his right boot? It's twisted and still in the regular stirrup. If he can't get that boot out of the stirrup, then he is in for some trouble.

Finally, did you notice that neither stunt man wore spurs? Or that the reins from the horses go back into the wagon and stagecoach where someone is driving the runaways? Or that in the Bob Steele photo, the handle on the right hand front corner of the wagon is so that the stuntman can pull himself into the front of the wagon and stop the horses?

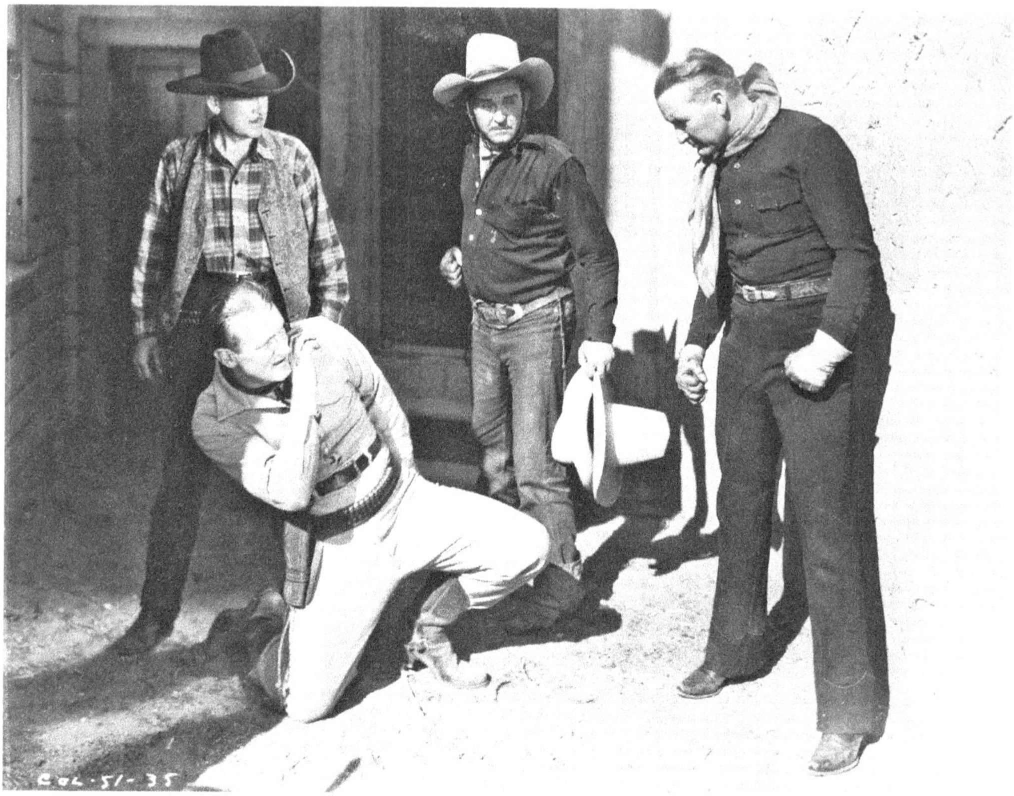

The Western Film Stills

Our subject this time is Tim McCoy. Tim portrayed more people of different ethnic groups than any other western actor that I knew of. He played a Mexican in *Border Caballero* (Puritan, 1936) and in *Lightning Carson Rides Again* (Victory, 1938). In *Six Gun Trail* (Victory, 1938) he played the part of a Chinese and then went back to the part of a Mexican in *Code of the Cactus* (Victory, 1939). Tim played a Gypsy in *Trigger Fingers* (Victory, 1939) and then returned to the part of a Mexican in *The Fighting Renegade* (Victory, 1939). Tim was better known for his roles at Columbia in the 1930s and as one of the Rough Riders with Buck Jones and Raymond Hatton in the '40s.

Our first photo (opposite top) shows Tim in a two-fisted role (literally) from *The Westerner* (Columbia, 1934). Tim gets the best of Joseph Sauers (later Joe Sawyer) while Hooper Atchley and Bud Osborne look on. The second photo (opposite bottom) shows Tim playing the role of a Chinese from the movie *Six Gun Trail* (Victory, 1938) with Nora Lane and Ben Corbet. Did you notice that Ben is wearing the latest fashion from the Far East? Tim played this role one time and it looks like he may have been wearing a wig. Note how the hair sticks out behind Tim's ear.

In the third photo (above), Tim is playing the part of a Gypsy in *Trigger Fingers* (Victory, 1939) as he shows a card trick to Jill Martin and John Elliott.

In the fourth photo (above) Tim is back to using his fists in *Fighting Renegade* (Victory, 1939) with Ted Adams on the receiving end. This was one of five movies in which Tim played the part of a Mexican.

Let's look at the photos of Tim playing a Gypsy and a Mexican. In each role Tim is wearing the same hat at the same angle and the same chin strap. Also the same mustache and the same sideburns pointed toward the front. Tim had nerve. Look at the shirt and vest he wore as a Gypsy. I wonder what they looked like in color.

Now look at all four pictures and remember the little quirk that some actors have regarding camera angles. I thought this rather interesting so I looked through a picture book about Tim. Out of 132 pictures of Tim, 36 showed his right side, 20 showed him straight on and 76 showed his left side.

A struggle between good and evil as Richard Powers has Roy Barcroft in an interesting position. Powers made a series of Western movies at RKO, Crescent and Monogram under the *nom de screen* Tom Keene before changing his name to Powers and playing supporting parts. He had the lead in this serial, *Desperados of the West* (Republic, 1950).

Barcroft is backed up against a large saw blade that was used in saw mills to cut up logs. Now look at Powers: He forgot to put a belt in his pants. And look at his gun. The grip is covered with tape. Even Barcroft's gun looks better. And is Barcroft trying to copy Hopalong Cassidy with his gloves tucked under his gun belt?

Did You Notice?

This time look for something that is the same in each picture. In the first photo (above) we find that our hero Bob Allen and the heroine Martha Tibbetts have been captured by outlaws dressed as Indians (left to right, Bob Kortman, Bud Osborne and Walter Miller). The wardrobe manager must have found a good sale on checkered shirts, but that is not what we are looking for. This scene is from *Ranger Courage* (Columbia, 1936).

The second picture (opposite) is from *Pioneer Trail* (Columbia, 1938). Jack Luden and Hal Taliaferro on the right seem to be having a disagreement. Hal has an unusual belt and in the shadow on the right, what is that circle of light? Whatever it is, it's not what we are looking for.

The Western Film Stills

The third picture (page 38) is from In *Early Arizona* (Columbia, 1938) with Gordon (Bill) Elliott pointing his finger at cigar-chewing Bud Osborne. The rest of the players are (left to right) Art Davis, Charles King, Al Ferguson, Franklyn Farnum and Harry Woods. Now look closely at Bob Allen, Jack Luden and Bill Elliott. Are they all wearing the same gun belt, holsters and guns? The gun belt is a little different from most gun belts. The part of the belt where the holster fits onto the belt is longer; it extends in front of and behind the holster. The buckle and the lacing is the same in each photo. To be sure if all the gun belts and holsters are the same, you would need to look at the carving on each piece.

Did You Notice?

One answer could be that all of the films of Bob Allen, Jack Luden and the first four of Bill Elliott's movies were produced by Columbia's Larry Darmour. He or the studio could have furnished the gun belt, holsters and guns. After Elliott's first four films, Columbia took over the production and Bill switched his holsters and then his guns were in the reverse position which he maintained for the rest of his western films.

When a cowboy got established, he could be identified a lot of times by his gun belt. By the way, did you notice that each of our heroes is wearing the same type of gloves?

In the days of the B Western movie the hero could be counted on not to smoke, use profanity or drink anything harder than sarsaparilla or buttermilk. He also kept his clothes on except barrel-chested George O'Brien who sometimes lost his shirt in a fight. This code of conduct extended to the hero's sidekick. Gabby Hays would come out with "You're darn tootin,'" but that was hardly profane.

In our photos we seem to be saying that there was some smoking going on. In the photo of Sunset Carson, he is rolling his own cigarette. Actually Sunset did not smoke in his movies at Republic. This is a publicity photo. Perhaps Republic wanted to publicize Sunset's ability to roll a cigarette like a real cowboy.

The second photo (above) is of Bob Allen from his Ranger series at Columbia. Bob did not smoke in any of his movies. This photo is from *The Unknown Ranger* (Columbia, 1936). As to why the studio would have Bob smoking in its advertising and not in the movie, I have no idea.

The third photo (above) is of one of the all-time favorites of the B western, Buck Jones. This picture is of a one-sheet poster and you can see that Buck has a lit cigarette in his mouth. Actually Buck did not smoke in this movie but he did smoke in a couple of other movies. The smoking could have been to entice adults into the movie, but smoking was usually not allowed for the hero.

The transfer of a person from a horse to the buckboard or stagecoach was always a thrill. There was also some danger in doing this stunt. One way to make the stunt less dangerous was to have the buckboard or stagecoach travel at a constant speed. To do this, the vehicle was not drawn by horses: It would be tied to the rear end of the camera car which would be driven at a constant speed which made the transfer easier. The rider still had to rely on his horse not to go too fast or slow or stumble, so there were some risks in this stunt.

In one picture we see Bob Steele or his double surprise Marion Weldon in *Colorado Kid* (A.W. Hackel, 1937). In the bottom right you can see the cross bar with the hook that usually has the leather strip that connects to the rigging on the horse.

In the picture from the Three Mesquiteers entry *Gangs of Sonora* (Republic, 1937), we have two transfers onto the stagecoach, Bob Livingston on the right and Bob Steele on the left. Notice how the men conceal their faces so that you don't know if it's the star or a stuntman. Steele is standing on something above his stirrup, which is down below. The something is an L-shaped stirrup fitted above the regular stirrup, making it easier to do the stunt. There are no horses to pull the stagecoach, the camera car is doing the pulling. In both pictures, someone is on the camera car holding onto the other end of the reins that would be attached to the horses.

Did You Notice?

Tim McCoy is holding off some villains (players unidentified) while protecting Lois January in the movie *Border Caballero* (Puritan, 1936). Tim is dressed as a Mexican. He did this several times in his movies and also played a Gypsy in one movie and a Chinese man in another. Look at the picture on the wall between Tim and the villains: That picture today, in good condition, would be very valuable.

The second picture (opposite) is from a Jack Perrin movie. Jack is holding his horse while his young friend (actor unidentified) is brushing the horses hooves. The thing we are looking for is the box that Jack is sitting on: Old Mr. Boston Apricot Nectar. That's a new one on me.

In both of these movies we have products being advertised. Did the companies pay the studios to place these objects in a movie as they do today? These movies were made primarily for the juvenile audience, which would not be drinking beer (we hope), and I don't think they would care much for apricot nectar. Most likely the set designer just used whatever was handy. By the way, did you notice Jack Perrin's pants? They have a strap that goes under the instep of the boots which hold his pant leg down. Also, his boots are the lace-up type, not the regular cowboy boots.

Did You Notice?

Our subject this time is kissing, a taboo subject for a lot of kids during their elementary school days. It was a common saying that cowboys did not kiss the girl but did kiss his horse. It was true that a majority of the B western actors did not kiss the girl. A hug, a look into her eyes and then the fadeout. But there were exceptions! In one picture we see Bob Steele planting one on this girl. Bob did this several times. He was about the same size as some of the girls in his movies. But did you ever see the Durango Kid or "Rocky" Lane kiss the girl?

The second photo (opposite) is from *Hellfire* (Republic, 1949). William Elliott and Marie Windsor are about to complete the business at hand. Marie seems to be into it more than Bill. This was considered a B+ or A- movie depending on which expert you read. Apparently it was okay to kiss in the more expensive movies but not the movies with a cheap budget. Finally, did you notice the footstool that Bill and Marie are seated on? Did they have furniture like that in the 1800s?

The Western Film Stills

Did You Notice?

The first picture (above) is from *Gun Town*, one of the movies Kirby Grant made for Universal in 1945–46. You can tell that Kirby is riding at a good clip if you noticed the horse's mane and Kirby's vest. Kirby has an unusual expression on his face. I presume that he's trying to keep the dust out of his eyes.

Did you notice the shadow of the horse and rider in the lower right hand corner? The shadow is what makes this picture interesting. This scene must have been shot early in the morning or late in the afternoon to get the shadow.

The second photo (opposite) is from the same movie and shows Kirby about to pull the trigger and he has the same squinting expression as before. Two unusual things for the hero: Kirby is wearing a vest and that was more common with the villains. He also has a ring where the wedding ring is worn.

The Western Film Stills

The lariat was an essential tool of the cowboy in real life and was used by some of the movie cowboys. Using the lariat to catch a crook was more prevalent in the early movies than it was in the movies toward the end of the B movie era.

One photo is from *The Vigilantes Are Coming* (Republic, 1936). Bob Livingston on the left has let fly his lariat at John Merton on the rock. Looks like Bob will get his man as the rope is about to settle over Merton. The person throwing the rope may not be Bob. Men who were experts at roping would hire out to different studios to do this type of thing. This also saved the movie cowboy countless hours learning how to use a rope.

The second picture is from *Ghost Town Riders* (Universal, 1938). This looks like how *not* to rope a rider off of his horse: I don't think the lariat will make it to the horseman on the left. Bob Baker had the lead in this movie but the lantern-jawed man in Bob's clothes does not look like Bob.

Did You Notice?

Tim McCoy (with gun) is exterminating the bad element in the movie *Outlaw Deputy* (Puritan Pictures, 1935). He's already got two on the ground and one on the sidewalk behind him. Si Jenks on the left is pointing out another one. Tim is wearing his badge and light-colored shirt instead of his usual dark shirt.

Did you notice that the two men on the ground made sure they fell between the horse droppings? Nora Lane is also avoiding the droppings. She had made several westerns by this time so she should have been an expert on the subject.

The photographer should have turned his camera a little to the right and he might have avoided the utility pole on the left in the background.

The Western Film Stills

The law (Bob Steele, center) has the situation well in hand in the movie *Ambush Trail* (PRC, 1946). It was part of a four-picture series that was Bob's *last* starring series. He had starred in movies since the silent days. The sheriff on the left is Ed Cassidy, who played all kind of parts. In the back is Syd Saylor who played comic roles (some not that funny) and on the right is I. Stanford Jolley who played a lot of villains.

Usually the hero in the B Western movie was clean-shaven but Bob is supporting a mustache. The story is that Bob needed it for a part coming up *The Big Sleep*, in a Humphrey Bogart picture at Warners, and he was not going to shave off his mustache for a B western and maybe lose the part at Warners. Everyone in this photo has a mustache except Saylor and he has whiskers all over.

Did You Notice?

The Western Film Stills

These two scenes are from the serial *King of the Royal Mounted* (Republic, 1940) with Allan Lane before he became Red Ryder and "Rocky" Lane. This scene is at a sawmill with Sgt. King lying on the belt that feeds the log into the large saw blade. Sgt. King has turned onto his side and sees the saw blade. The saw blade is not turning so he's in no danger in this scene.

In the second picture King is on his stomach and the blade is now spinning (the teeth are a blur). King's fingers on his left hand are a little close to the blade.

Did You Notice?

This scene is from *Cowboy from Sundown* (Monogram, 1940) with Tex Ritter in the center pointing his finger. The judge at the hotel desk is Slim Andrews who became Tex's sidekick Arkansas Slim Andrews. The person seated on the stairs landing is Roscoe Ates and on the far right in profile is Glenn Strange.

In this courtroom scene there are 34 people. Some women wore hats (or bonnets) but not the men. Men were to remove all headgear when court was in session. Well, two guys forgot to follow the director's instructions. Right in the center is a man with his hat on, and in front of the door on the left is another.

This scene is from *West of Carson City* (Universal 1940) with Johnny Mack Brown (center) and Bob Baker (left). Bob is wearing an interesting costume: He is wearing chaps and his holster is attached to the chaps. Only time I ever saw this.

Johnny has corralled Bob and someone who appears to have a pack of cigarettes in his shirt pocket. Look in the background on the right and you will see a light fixture and pole that should have been out of sight.

After his days in the movies were over, Baker made his living designing and carving different things in leather. I suspect that he designed and made his chaps and holsters that you see in this photo.

Did You Notice?

We might subtitle these two pictures Small Things. The first is of the Three Mesquiteers Max Terhune, Ray Corrigan and Bob Livingston. The kid on the left is Sammy McKim, who made several movies with the Mesquiteers. Sammy is small but that is not what I'm referring to. Sammy is holding on to his rifle but in case he needs backup all he has to do is reach into his hip pocket and pull out his slingshot.

The second photo is from *Indian Territory* (Columbia, 1950) with Gene Autry restraining James Griffith. What is small in this picture? You will find it just above Griffith's holster on his right side: a book of matches which I do not believe were invented yet during the time period of this movie. A box of matches maybe, but not book matches. Griffith most likely used the matches to light a cigarette and forgot that he put the matches in his belt when the still photographer took this picture.

Did You Notice?

Tom Tyler has come to the rescue, dragging an unidentified player from a burning building. Notice the victim is not about to give up his rifle in the movie *Tracey Rides* (Reliable, 1935). The fire by the door looks like they threw some kerosene on the wall and put a match to it. Observing the action is a cow on the right and up on the hill on the right are two men seated. Further down and to the left is another man sitting on the ground with a pole. Perhaps these people lived in the area and wanted to watch the moviemakers, or they were to come down the hill if the fire got out of hand. But they are sure not supposed to be in the picture.

The Great Adventures of Wild Bill Hickok (Columbia 1937) was the first starring movie for Bill Elliott, and the "Wild Bill" from the title stuck. Bill became known as Will Bill Elliott throughout his Columbia movies and his first series at Republic. In this picture, Bill is pulling his horse to a stop. However, the gun on his left side has come flying out of its holster on his left side. You can see the gun upside down just to the right of the holster.

The old Monogram barn must have been used in over a hundred movies. It was actually two barns in one.

In the first photo (opposite, top) we have Bob Baker teasing Don Barclay in *Outlaw Express* (Universal, 1938). The barn is supposed to be logs but it's actually boards with caulking between the boards. On Bob's buckskin shirt, notice the zipper on the left side. Sure makes it easier to change.

In the second photo (opposite) we can see the front of the barn in the movie *Riders of the Frontier* (Monogram, 1939). Tex Ritter has roped a couple of varmints. Hal Taliaferro is to the left of Ritter's horse and Mantan Moreland has his hands in his pockets. From a distance, the exterior of the barn looks like logs.

In *Raiders of the South* (Monogram, 1947), Johnny Mack Brown and Marshall Reed are into boxing. Raymond Hatton (with pole) is the referee. John Merton is looking after the ladies Evelyn Brent and Reno Blair. The barn is the same one as in the first two pictures, only this time it's the opposite end of the barn. This end has vertical siding, no logs.

Did You Notice?

Bulldogging was one of the stunts that was used a lot in the B western. Before the actual bulldogging took place, there was a lot of chasing by a rider trying to catch up with another rider. When the rider catches up with the first rider, he then leaps from his horse to the back of the other rider and pulls him off of his horse.

The first photo is from the movie *Tenting Tonight on the Old Camp Grounds* (Universal, 1943): Johnny Mack Brown has just pulled Tex Ritter off of his horse. Actually, stunt doubles are doing this scene. In the second picture, Ritter has just bulldogged Brown off of *his* horse, and that kind of evens it up. This scene is from *Little Joe the Wrangler* (Universal, 1942). In this stunt the stuntmen are falling onto soft ground. Notice that the men are not wearing spurs.

Did You Notice?

In *Wolf Riders* (Reliable, 1935) Jack Perrin is trying to hold off Slim Whitaker while the Indians have William Gould (hands raised) corralled in the background. The odd thing in this picture is that Jack is holding his right hand like he's holding a gun. Jack! No gun, make a fist, like Slim Whitaker.

The second picture (opposite) from an unknown film has Bob Baker in some kind of trouble. Bob's adversary (actor unidentified) is holding Bob's leg, but why? The villain has a gun but it's not doing him much good pointing away from Bob. Bob has his hands up and that does not make much sense as he could reach down and draw a gun very easily. These two pictures are unusual.

The Western Film Stills

Did You Notice?

    This scene is from one of Charles Starrett's movies for Columbia. The story is set in Canada, but this scene was filmed at the Columbia Ranch in Burbank, California.

    This building at the end of the street was usually a courthouse in the Western movies. In this scene it was the office of the Royal Canadian Mounted Police. The extras are dressed like it is the cool weather of Canada, so for their sake I hope it was cool in Southern California. How about the sign on the front at the second story, 1861 A. D.? I wonder if they changed that sign with each movie. On the far left you can see light poles and wires in the background.

The Western Film Stills

Our three-in-one photo goes back to the days when the studios gave the public three cowboys in one movie. These three were known as the Range Busters: John King, David Sharpe and Max Terhune. Ray Corrigan had been with this trio but then, as I understand it, there was a dispute over money and David Sharpe filled in for Corrigan in a few movies. This scene is from *Trail Riders* (Monogram, 1942).

This scene was taken at the Jauregui Ranch. The barn in the background and the corral on the left are gone along with the rest of the buildings on the ranch. In the background just to the right of Max Terhune's gun there's an automobile under the tree in the shade.

A photo depicting a fight from the serial *Mystery Mountain* (Mascott, 1934). Ken Maynard (left) has knocked down the villain (actor unidentified) but when Ken went after him the villain drew back his feet and then pushed Ken toward the edge of the cliff. But there's nothing to worry about: Tarzan, Ken's horse, is on the job. Did you notice the rope from Tarzan to the ground and over the cliff? All Ken has to do is grab the rope and hold on. Then Ken will whistle and Tarzan will pull him up. By then, of course the villain will be gone.

The Western Film Stills

This confusing scene is from *Guns for Hire* (Kent, 1932) with Lane Chandler about to use his rifle on the head of Ben Corbett, who seems to be anticipating the blow. Lawman Yakima Canutt is standing in the doorway but what is he doing? With all the action going on, Yak is looking at the floor and also has his gun pointed at the floor. Looking for a target?

At one time it was thought that either Lane Chandler or Gary Cooper would be the next big movie star. It's rather obvious who won out. Chandler in the early thirties starred in 13 independent westerns of dubious quality. He had supporting roles for many years after his starring days.

This is a group shot from *Drifting Along* (Monogram, 1946). At the gambling table is Ted Mapes on the left and Marshall Reed smoking the cigarette. They don't seem to appreciate the singing. Smith Ballew (no hat) is the lead singer. His group is Curt Barrett and the Trails men. By the way, how could you *not* notice those chaps? Only entertainers or comedians could dress like that.

The Western Film Stills

In the Gilbert Roland series of Cisco Kid films, Roland seemed to be right in place, as did the cigarette: Roland played Cisco as a laid-back semi-outlaw hero. His costume with the straw hat and the over-the-shoulder garment was part of his makeup. In some films he seemed to smoke cigarettes in most every dialogue scene. He would stick the cigarette behind his ear before a fight and then start smoking it again after the fight — without relighting it. Some kids (including me) must have wondered why his hair did not catch fire. This scene is from *South of Monterey* (Monogram, 1946).

The Western Film Stills

Two pictures shot in the same spot for the movie *The Vanishing Outlaw* (Western Adventures, 1951) which starred Lash LaRue and Fuzzy St. John. The people in the pictures are the movie's villains. In the first photo, the man on the left is House Peters Jr. I don't know his mean-looking partner.

In the second picture everyone is up on their feet. House is now loading his gun and his partner is still mad. It's easy to see that these two pictures were taken at the same place. On the left side you can see the hole in the rock and in the rock, on the right there is a curved mark like a horseshoe.

These two pictures are from the feature *In Old Santa Fe* (Mascot, 1934). In one picture, Ken Maynard and Gene Autry are shaking hands. In the other picture, Gene is playing the guitar and Smiley Burnett is playing the accordion. These two pictures were obviously taken at the same place. The shape of the cactus is the same in both pictures. In the picture with Maynard, Gene Autry does not have a gun belt. In the picture with Burnett, Autry now has a gun belt, and the belt and gun look very much like the one that Maynard was wearing in the *first* picture.

Did You Notice?

This is an interesting situation in the movie *Law and Lead* (Colony, 1936) with Rex Bell on the floor. The man with the advantage is Wally Wales, later Hal Taliaferro. Wally starred in silent and talkies until 1935. He then played supporting parts until 1952. Bell made a few movies after this then went to Nevada where he had a clothing store before going into politics. He was married to Clara Bow. If I was Rex Bell, I would not be pulling on Wally's legs. What if Wally pulled the trigger? What a way to go.

It looks like Tom Tyler (with black hat and rifle) is accusing Slim Whitaker (right) of some evil deed. John Elliott (next to Whitaker) has his gun on Slim to reinforce the point. Seated is Robert McKenzie as the sheriff, who looks none too happy. This is from the movie *Ridin' On* (Reliable, 1936).

Did you ever see a desk like the sheriff's? It looks like a big wooden box resting on some piano legs. Should be in the Smithsonian.

Did You Notice?

Hoot Gibson (in buckskin) has two long barrel six-guns and is holding this gang at bay in a scene from *Cavalcade of the West* (First Division, 1936). Hoot is supported by Marion Shilling on his right and Nina Guilbert on his left. The man in the center in the back is Earl Dwire and next to him is Budd Buster. Left of center, being held back, is Rex Lease.

If Hoot can't hold off this gang, he can turn to his right, run a few feet, get in the car and move out: In the upper right hand corner you can see part of a tire, fender and bumper.

It was always great to see our cowboy heroes perform tricks with their horses. In this photo we can see Bob Allen in the movie *Ranger Courage* (Columbia, 1937) putting his horse through its paces. Bob has a hold on the reins but the horse is taking his cues from the trainer on the far right who is using hand signals. There are utility poles on the right in the background.

Did You Notice?

This scene has Bob Baker about to throw a villain. Glenn Strange (on the left) has just socked Jack Rockwell and Carleton Young on the right is about to throw a piece of wood at Baker. I don't know the two that are wrestling in the center. Did you notice that the person Bob Baker is about to throw is looking around to see where he will land? He also has his legs and arms crossed so when he goes flying he won't hit anyone with his boots or arms. This action scene is from *Guilty Trail* (Universal, 1938).

Three friends in conversation on a western street from the silent film *The Vanishing West* (Mascot, 1928): Jack Perrin (center) went on to make talking pictures as the star and later played supporting parts. On the right is Yakima Canutt who seems to be happy about his money. Notice the blocking of the head gear is different from what you would see in the forties. Yak is wearing chaps and no one could ever mistake these chaps for their own: Under Yak's left hand you can see his name that has been carved into the leather. I don't know the man on the left or like his lipstick.

I used this picture when I was trying to identify the gun belt and holster set of Bob Allen and other Columbia western stars. Again this scene is from *Ranger Courage* (Columbia, 1937) with (left to right) Bob Kortman, Bob Allen, Bud Osborne, Martha Tibbetts and Walter Miller. After the checkerboard bandits get tired of keeping the ranger and the lady apart, they can all have a drink and one can sit down: On the right, behind the wagon wheel, you can see a barrel with a spigot sitting on a chair. Whoever gets there first can have the canvas-back chair in the background on the far right.

The Western Film Stills

A fight? Almost, but looks like Lash LaRue will not be punching Jim Bannon, who had been around in supporting parts for awhile. The following year he started his Red Ryder series. He then went back to second lead parts.

This scene is from *Frontier Revenge* (Screen Guild, 1948). Ray Bennett in the center is breaking up the misunderstanding. Later Lash made a movie called *King of the Bullwhip* (Western Adventure, 1951) and this became like a title for him. At the time he made the movie *Frontier Revenge* they could have given him a title: King of the Belt Buckles!

Did You Notice?

A Whip Wilson double feature: The first photo (above) is from *In Shadows of the West* (Monogram, 1949) and Whip is paying off Riley Hill while Andy Clyde and Reno Brown look on. Hill played second lead to almost everyone at Monogram in hopes of being the star someday but he never made it. The second picture (opposite) from *Abilene Trail* (Monogram, 1951). Whip and Andy are helping Tommy Farrell who seems to have some kind of ailment. Now Whip has his whip on the right side and the three are all left-handed gunslingers. Whoever printed this photo turned the negative over so the picture wrongly shows the three to be left-handed.

The Western Film Stills

Did You Notice?

The gunfight is in progress as Russell Hayden (right) and Bob Wills (left) look for targets. I think the people in the back are in Bob's group, The Texas Playboys. If Bob decides to shoot, I hope he raises his gun up a little, otherwise he will be shooting the back of the table. Would that table really protect you from a bullet? If the gunfight gets too fierce, Russell, Bob and the rest of the gang can turn around and run down the walk and jump into the truck.

In the credits at the bottom of the picture it says Bob Wills and His Texas Playboys and Russell Hayden in *The Lone Prairie* (Columbia, 1942). I wonder what Russell Hayden thought about that.

Looks like the hair dresser just combed everyone's hair.

The Western Film Stills

The three men (Raymond Hatton and two unidentified actors) posing for this picture seem to be saying, "Okay, make your play!" The one on the right has made a small target of himself and is drawing a bead on someone. The guy on the left has almost no protection. Perhaps he wants as much exposure as possible, hoping for a speaking part in his next film. He is also wearing his wedding ring. Hatton (center) seems not to be concerned about anything. His six-gun has one long barrel.

The wrangler in the background is not concerned with the problems of the three gunfighters: He has to see that the horses are ready to go into action when called for. This photo is from *Gun Talk* (Monogram, 1947).

Did You Notice?

In the western film, the hero has to have a nice-looking horse and be able to ride it. In the movie *In Old Mexico* (Monogram, 1945) we see Duncan Renaldo as the Cisco Kid riding along one of the chase roads at Corriganville. Duncan is riding from the far end of the ranch toward the town set. The ravine on the left was used in several non–Western movies.

How can anyone not notice the pipe railing in the foreground? It's part of the camera truck. The photographer centered his subject but got part of the railing in the picture.

Smith Ballew (standing, holding his coat) was the star of *Hawaiian Buckaroo* (Principal–20th Century–Fox, 1938). It is true that Hawaii had cattle ranches and the cowboys were called Paneolas, but his film was made in California. To create the feeling of being in Hawaii, the cowboys have flowers in their hat bands. This would not be done in Hawaii except at some kind of celebration. The man on horseback in the center is wearing a shirt that Hawaiian working men wore out of doors. Also, cowboys in Hawaii did not wear gun belts.

Did You Notice?

This has to be one of the most unusual still photos taken to advertise a Western movie. In the foreground is villain Karl Hackett (left) and one of his henchmen (unidentified actor). The man standing on his horse is our hero Fred Scott. Fred was athletic but he could not make this jump; that would be a record in the standing broad jump. This is a scene from the movie *Rangers Roundup* (Spectrum, 1938).

Looks like the U.S. Cavalry has caught up with the Cisco Kid and Pancho (Duncan Renaldo, middle and Leo Carrillo, left) in the movie *The Gay Amigo* (UA, 1949). Joe Sawyer (right) and Cisco decided to settle their differences man to man and Cisco has just delivered a knockout punch to Joe. Pancho did not do much fighting, instead warning his partner or offering encouragement. Before he got slugged, Joe should have called time and removed the wristwatch he was wearing.

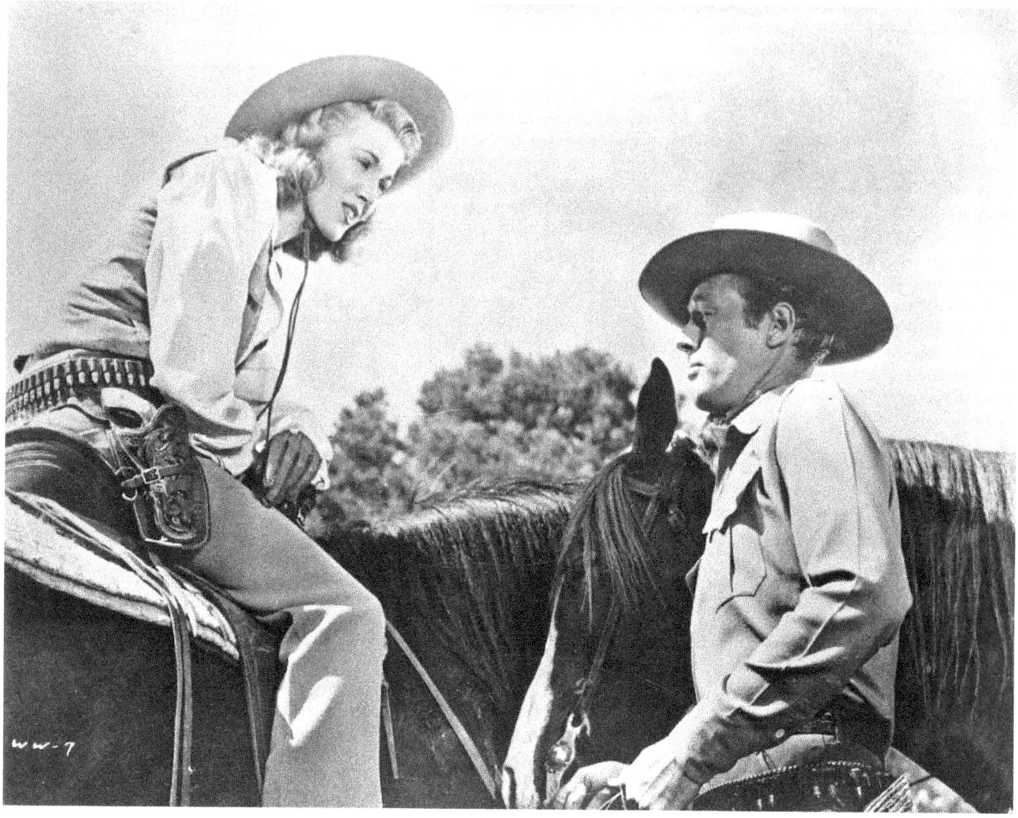
WW-7

FELIZ
THOMAS HA
ASSISTA
U.S. ATTO
GENE
LAW PR

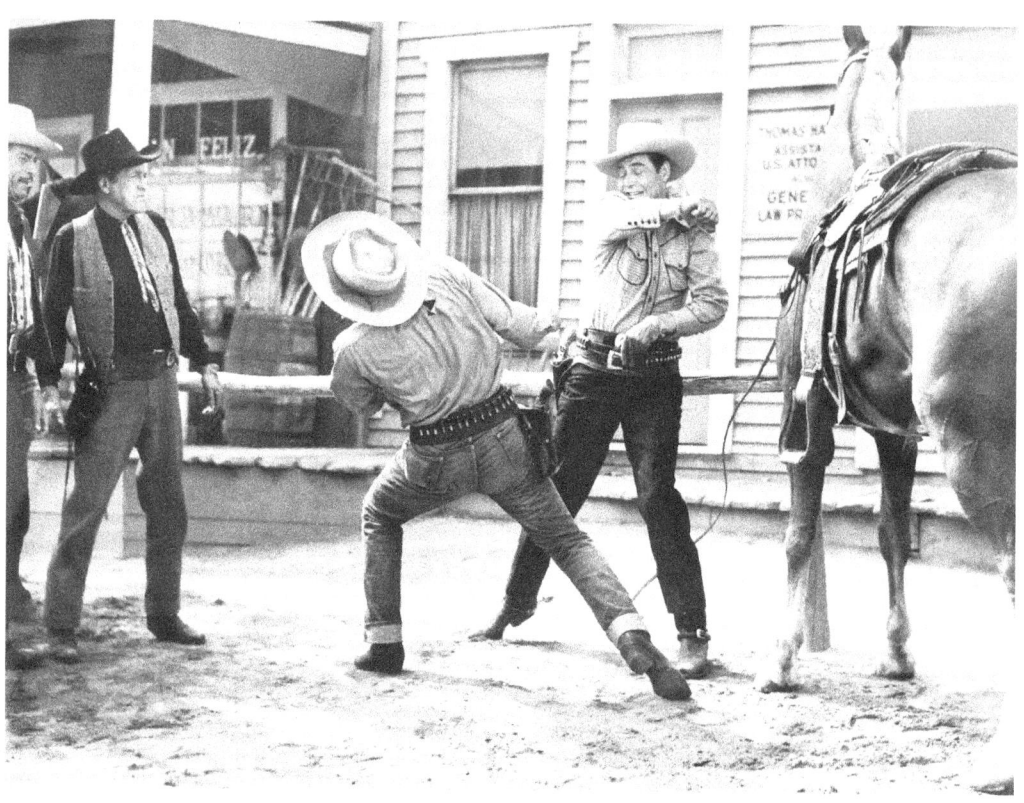

The Western Film Stills

In *Wanderer of the Wasteland* (RKO, 1945) Audrey Long is talking to James Warren who appears to have his eyes shut. The photographer took the picture just as Jim blinked. Audrey's pistol looks small for her holster but she might have trouble with a regular size six-gun.

The second picture is from *Desert Vigilante* (Columbia, 1949). Charles Starrett has just busted one of the villains (actor unidentified) with his eyes closed. Again he blinked, but it's a heck of a picture to put out for kids to see, the hero hitting a guy with his own eyes closed. The two guys on the left are old timers, I. Stanford Jolley and George Chesebro. George started in movies in silent days.

Did You Notice?

Tim Holt is running down the street trying to make a quick mount onto his horse in the movie *Cyclone on Horseback* (RKO, 1941). Notice how he is pulling out part of the saddle so he can put his left foot into the stirrup. Ray Whitley is leading Tim's horse while Lee "Lasses" White looks on. I wonder if Tim made it on this try.

The Western Film Stills

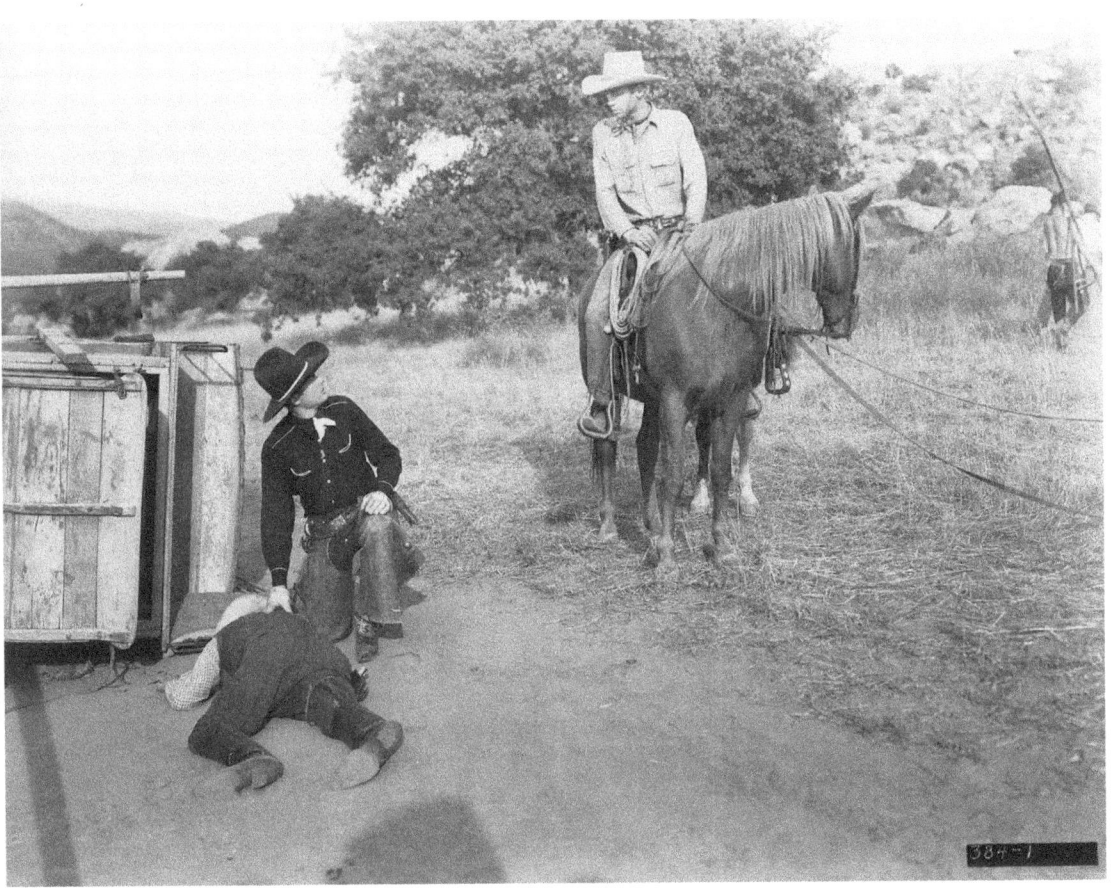

In a scene from *Ghost Town Riders* (Universal, 1938), Bob Baker is checking out the man on the ground who must have been on the stagecoach when it turned over on its side. He is also talking to Hank Worden (on horseback), who is holding onto some long reins. The two or three men on the far right are not concerned about this scene, they are getting ready for the next one. Hurry up, the sun's getting low!

Did You Notice?

This time we have three cowboys jumping their horses over a wooden fence. The three cowboys are the Three Mesquiteers, Max Terhune, John Wayne and Ray Corrigan, in a scene from *Santa Fe Stampede* (Republic, 1938). This is a good action shot but did you notice that it's not Terhune, Wayne or Corrigan on horseback doing the jumping? It's their doubles on their horses doing the jumping. It could be that the horses are doubles also. Not all horses could jump very well.

The second picture (opposite) shows Mesquiteers Terhune, Wayne and Corrigan at the hitching rack. Their costumes are similar to what you see on the three on horseback. But Max Terhune's hat at the hitching rack is not the same as it is in the jumping scene.

The Western Film Stills

The star of *Riders of Rio* (Round Up Pictures, 1931) was Lane Chandler. Here he is having a good laugh at something. Could it be the boards he is examining? Maybe he figured out what the letters say if you put them together in the right order. I tried for three days, and no luck. But I did notice the light pole in the background which would not have been there in the time frame of this movie

The Western Film Stills

The star of *Rio Grande Patrol* (RKO, 1950) is Tim Holt (center). Tim has lost his guns and is waiting to see what the two villains want him to do, stay in the U.S. or step over into Mexico. The man on horseback behind Tim is Tom Tyler, who starred in silent and sound movies. He made fifty talking pictures as the star, then played supporting parts on both sides of the law before coming back to the good guy side in the last 13 films in the Three Mesquiteers series. From there it was secondary parts in over thirty films.

Jack Perrin (left) starred in silent and sound movies through 1936. He then moved into supporting parts. When he did these parts, he dressed about the same as when he was the lead in the movie. Sometimes he would be dressed better then the star.

In *Trouble in Sundown* (RKO, 1939), George O'Brien in his denim outfit is being restrained while Ward Bond is being held back by Perrin who is wearing the same hat and gun belt that he wore when he was the star in a movie. He did change to a nice plaid shirt. Chill Wills is in the back center.

In *Land of the Six Guns* (Monogram, 1940) Jack Randall (right) has the drop on Perrin (left) and Carl Mathews. Perrin is again wearing the same hat, gun belt and shirt he wore as a star. The only difference in his appearance is the vest he is wearing. Sometimes wearing a vest almost identifies one as a villain. This scene was filmed at Bronson Canyon.

Did You Notice?

It was a hot day when they filmed this scene for *Riders of Pasco Basin* (Universal, 1940) with Johnny Mack Brown here taking on two of the villains (actors unidentified). They must be the brains of the outlaw element: Both are wearing suits. Johnny has sweated through his shirt under his arm but also look at the front of his shirt: wet spots almost down to this belt buckle.

Fred Scott is singing for his supper in this scene from *Melody of the Plains* (Spectrum, 1937). Al St. John is strumming the guitar and David Sharpe in black hat and white shirt is resting under a tree on the right. This scene was filmed at the Walker Ranch; the clue is the sycamore trees with the white bark and the stream bed behind the group. It was usually dry but would have water during the winter months.

These characters are waiting for something to eat but the cook is enjoying Fred's singing and has nothing in his mixing bowl. And if he *had* something mixed up, there is no fire in the campfire to cook it. Never mind, they will all get box lunches from the movie company.

Did You Notice?

It's a time for singing and relaxing in *Chip of the Flying U* (Universal, 1939). In this picture Bob Baker is playing the guitar and singing. All the people around Bob are doing something you seldom see in a group photo: whistling. They are accompanying Bob on the song "Mr. Moon" by Everett Carter and Milt Rosen. The men around Bob are a musical group, The Texas Rangers. This scene was filmed at the actual bunkhouse on the Jauregui Ranch in Newhall, California.

Ray Corrigan (left) and Bob Livingston seem to be having a disagreement about the girl (Rita Cansino) in the Three Mesquiteers film *Hit the Saddle* (Republic, 1937). Ray is telling Bob not to get involved with a bar girl. Rita made a few westerns on her way to stardom under the name Rita Hayworth.

Did You Notice?

These two pictures are from the movie *Terror of the Plains* (Reliable, 1934) which starred Tom Tyler. In the first picture Tom is on the ground and behind him his partner Frank Rice is preventing a villain (actor unidentified) from shooting Tom with his rifle. On the left, William Gould has restrained Slim Whitaker from shooting Tom with a six-gun.

In the second picture on the left Frank Rice. Someone is holding Slim again while Tom has just landed a punch on Gould's chin. Nice way to pay back the favor in the first picture, Tom! The girl in the center is Roberta Gail.

These two pictures could have nothing to do with the storyline of the movie. The still photographer would often pose the actors, creating interesting shots that would draw kids into the theater.

In the movie *Murder in the Clouds* (First National, 1934), Lyle Talbot is being untied by a man with very long pants — he would be in style today. The man in his vest is Wheeler Oakman and the gun-wielding man on the left is Gordon Elliott with a mustache. The two law officers on the left are dressed the same except for their holsters. Wardrobe must not have been able to find two holsters that matched. This was a small bit part for Elliott.

Ten years later you see Wild Bill Elliott, now a star at Republic, as he does a stunt that is usually left to the stunt person (stopping a runaway). By then Bill no longer had a mustache.

In westerns a lot of time was spent in saloons and the hero was usually a non-drinker. This scene is from *Code of the West* (RKO, 1947), with James Warren on the right. He played the lead in westerns and a few other movies before going back to his first profession, being an artist. The girl is Carol Forman who played in movies for some time. On the left is Raymond Burr, on his way up. He hit it big on TV when he was the star of *Perry Mason* and later *Ironside*. In the B western you would see people who had been stars but were now in small parts on their way down as well as people starting out who later became very well-known actors.

Sammy McKim (right) is pointing out something to his friends Eddy Waller and Phyllis Isley in the Three Mesquiteers film *New Frontier* (Republic, 1939). Sammy did juvenile parts in western and non–Western movies for several years. As an adult he worked as an artist for the Disney studio until he retired.

Waller made many movies over the years in supporting roles including the sidekick in some of the Allan Lane westerns. Phyllis Isley made a few films at Republic and then changed her name to Jennifer Jones. She went on to become a big star and also was awarded an Oscar for her performance in *The Song of Bernadette* (20th Century–Fox, 1943). She got her start in a B western.

Gene Autry has just wounded Bob Livingston in this shootout scene from *Riders in the Sky* (Columbia, 1949). Both of these men at one time starred in their own series at Republic. Livingston started at MGM in supporting roles and then moved to Republic where he played western and non-western parts. He played his last starring role in 1944 and then went into supporting parts until 1975.

Autry started at Mascot in 1936. Mascot became part of Republic and Autry starred there until he went into the service in World War II. After the war he moved to Columbia. Gene was still the star in films at this time while Bob was playing the villain in one of Gene's films.

Max Terhune with his dummy Elmer provided a lot of laughs for the audience while appearing in the Three Mesquiteers and Range Busters series and other assorted horse operas. Max was very good at card tricks. In several A movies you would see only his hands as he dealt the cards for someone else.

In this photo, Max and Elmer are dressed like father and son with the same shirt and bandana. The little thing that I noticed was the dice that keeps the bandanas secure around the neck.

Did You Notice?

These three were known as the Three Mesquiteers: Max Terhune, Bob Livingston and Ray Corrigan. Bob did sing in a couple of films and Ray and Max sang a song when they were in the Range Busters series. But none were known as singers so this trio that you see here was not a singing trio. Corrigan seems a little uncertain, Terhune is giving it his all and Livingston is just being himself.

Johnny Mack Brown, Fuzzy Knight and Bob Baker in one of the movies they did at Universal, *Bad Man from Red Butte*, (1940). Before this series, Bob had been the star in 12 westerns at Universal, but *this* was Johnny's series.

The facial expressions tell the story: Johnny is not enjoying this song. He did sing a song or two later in his career at Monogram but he was noted for action, not singing. Bob was a singer and from his expression he feels he could do a better job of singing then Fuzzy. Fuzzy's singing in Western movies was on the comical side, but in the color film *Trail of the Lonesome Pine* (1936) many tears were shed when he sang "Twilight on the Trail."

Did You Notice?

A scene from *Boot Hill Brigade* (1937). This is one of the A.W. Hackel pictures released through Republic Pictures. Everyone seems to be holding back two people that have a problem: Johnny Mack Brown on the right is held back by Horace Murphy and the kid Bobby Nelson. But it takes five men to hold onto the villain Dick Curtis. This was your lucky day, Johnny. This was filmed at the Jauregui Ranch with ranch house and picket fence in the background.

Gene Autry (left) restrains Russell Hayden, who has been wounded. Gene had the reputation of helping movie business people who had fallen on hard times. Hayden started out playing a young hothead partner in the Hopalong Cassidy series from 1937 through 1941. He then appeared a series with Charles Starrett and next had his own series at Columbia before a short series at Screen Guild and another at Lippert. He was now in secondary roles but later came back on TV with *Cowboy G Men*. So Russell started at the bottom, worked his way to the top, went back to supporting parts and then came back up on TV This scene is from *Valley of Fire* (Columbia, 1951).

Did You Notice?

In this scene from *The Crimson Trail* (Universal, 1935), Buck Jones is leaping from his horse to the villain. Note how the villain is bracing himself with his left leg and his arms are up to catch Buck before they fall to the ground. The ground has been dug up and leveled which makes for a much softer landing. Buck does not look like Buck, so we're probably seeing a stunt man. The girl is Polly Ann Young.

The Western Film Stills

Unknown Valley (Columbia, 1933) appears to have some kind of cult in the story. Buck Jones on the left is preventing Ward Bond from whipping the youngster tied to the post. Frank Ellis on the far right does not like Buck's interferences. Did you ever see such false bears? Cults have been around for a long time and we still have cults around over seventy years later.

We might say of these two pictures that the teeth have it: Charles Starrett is posing for a publicity picture with a four-legged friend on the back lot at the Columbia Ranch (which later became a strip mall). Note the utility poles in the background and a car or truck next to the building. This is from *Cattle Raiders* (Columbia, 1938).

The second photo (opposite) is from *Deep in the Heart of Texas* (Universal, 1942). Johnny Mack Brown and comedian Fuzzy Knight compare choppers with White Flash, who belonged to Tex Ritter, a co-star in this movie. Johnny and Fuzzy are dressed like dudes from the East.

Did You Notice?

PRC made a long series of western pictures with Buster Crabbe (center). Buster and Kermit Maynard (Ken's brother) are having at it as they usually did when they were in a movie together. This movie was filmed at Corriganville. They're fighting in front of was the general store; next was the stable and then the blacksmiths.

The two men watching the action are not there by accident. A number of people came to Corriganville every filming day to get into a scene, make a little money and get a free lunch.

The Western Film Stills

People going to a wedding in *Decision at Sundown* (Columbia, 1957) starred Randolph Scott. Randy is not in this scene. Could he be waiting at the church? John Litel is driving the buckboard alongside the bride Karen Steele. This scene was shot on the western set at the Columbia Ranch. The Lincoln Hotel was a saloon in some pictures and the building across the street was usually a bank. What you do not usually see is on the left up above the roof of the house: a bank of lights used for lighting a set on the next street.

Buffalo Bill Jr. (Jay Wilsey) on the left in a scene from one of his movies. He dominates the picture even though he is on the side. He is one step above the three men on the right and two steps below the girl in the center but he still makes all of them look like they are on the short side. With his cowboy boots and a hat that extends several inches above his head, our hero looks like one of today's seven-foot basketball players.

This is Don Barry in *Fugitive from Sonora* (Republic, 1943). That is some scar Don has on his right cheek. Sometimes he played the "outlaw" part better than he played his "good guy" parts. If Don has had enough of this, he can walk around the end of the wagon and take off in the truck parked under the tree in the background.

The group at the bar in the Silver Dollar Saloon (look at the mirror in the background) includes Edward Cassidy, Kenneth MacDonald, Richard Powers and Tim Holt. This scene is from *Storm Over Wyoming* (RKO, 1950). Using the name Tom Keene, Powers had starred in a series of westerns at RKO, then Crescent and finally at Monogram. His last starring film was at Monogram in 1942: *Where Trails End*. I guess Tom got the message as he changed his name and did supporting roles through 1958.

Looks like a showdown between three villains (all with dark hats) and our three-gun hero Kirby Grant in *Ban Men of the Border* (Universal, 1945). The three bad ones seated are Pierce Lyden, Roy Brent and Ed Howard. Kirby wore one gun, so he must have disarmed someone before this saloon scene. Heroes spent a lot of time in saloons even though they did not drink. There were no soda fountain in those days. If the hero wanted water, milk or sarsaparilla, this was the place.

Did You Notice?

Some people in the movies went from starring roles to supporting parts. From nice-looking to not-so-nice. In our first picture, Johnny Mack Brown has stopped the action in a gunfight. His sidekick Raymond Hatton is on the right, the actor in the middle is unidentified. Notice all the crud on the inside of the horse trough. Would you let your horse drink out of that? This photo is from *The Fighting Ranger* (Monogram, 1948).

The second picture (opposite) is from *Apache Uprising* (Paramount, 1966): a much heavier Johnny Mack Brown confronts Corinne Calvet. This movie featured several players who had been stars when they were younger. Seeing Brown as an overweight sheriff in '66 was a big disappointment to many fans.

Our hero Rex Lease is wearing jodhpurs and lace-up boots. The character may have been an Easterner who just came West. This scene must have been filmed early in the morning just as the sun came over the mountain (note the shadows). Charles "Slim" Whitaker (to the left of Rex) is pointing out something in the distance. Must have been a little chilly as most people have coats on.

A shot from *Son of a Gunfighter* (MGM, 1966), which starred Russ Tamblyn. Get the feeling that this film may have been made in Mexico? You can see the caballeros riding through the pass. Now the people on top are going to roll the wagon down onto the riders below. The wood and brush would be set afire. What we are looking for is under the wagon wheels: rails that will keep the wagon going straight ahead onto the unsuspecting riders below.

Did You Notice?

This scene is from *Robbers of the Range* (RKO, 1941) with Virginia Vale and Tim Holt. These two made several movies together before Tim went into the military during World War II. In this picture, it's all in the hands. As Tim grips Virginia's arm, you can see Band Aids on Tim's thumb and first finger. Did they have Band Aids in the 1890s? Also, would a frontier woman have long, manicured finger nails in those days?

The Western Film Stills

A scene from the movie *Ride 'Em Cowboy* (Universal, 1942), an Abbott and Costello spoof of the Old West in a modern setting at a dude ranch. Although Abbott and Costello were top-billed, two western stars got a lot of screen time, Johnny Mack Brown and Dick Foran. In the center of the photo is Costello mugging it up with Anne Guynne. Abbott is to the right in the checkerboard shirt trying to make time with the two girls in bathing suits. Just behind the two girls is Richard Lane in sports coat and hat. Over on the left in the back with the black hat is Ella Fitzgerald.

This movie also had a former western star in it. He had been a star at the same studio from 1937 to 1939 and then co-starred in another series through 1940. However, his part in the co-starring series was very small compared to that of his co-star. In this movie he is not listed in the credits and he does not have a word of dialogue. He can be seen in the background at the swimming pool and at the dance, but he is very obvious as the bus driver. You can see him in the photo on the far left as he leans out the window of the bus: It's Bob Baker. I wonder what his thoughts might have been ... from star to co-star to bit parts in five years.

The name of this movie can be found in this photo. Johnny Mack Brown (in the doorway with hand raised) has a chain from each of his shirt pockets with something hanging from the chain in the center. That object is the name of this movie: *The Silver Bullet* (Universal, 1942). Standing next to Johnny is Jennifer Holt, daughter of Jack Holt and sister of Tim Holt.

On the platform on the left are LeRoy Mason and Rex Lease. There are a lot of flat top hats in this election scene. Elections at this time could have been held in the saloon. Women were not allowed to vote at this time so they would not be going into the saloon unless they worked there.

The Western Film Stills

A fight scene from *West of Carson City* (Universal, 1940) with the fighting in a horizontal position. In the back, Bob Baker is on top of his opponent while in front Johnny Mack Brown is trying to keep the knife from doing any damage. This action is taking place on the barroom floor. You can see poker chips and cards in the back as well as cigarette butts and a cigar. Johnny is giving Bob some unintended help: He has his spur from his boot in the hair of Bob's adversary.

Two scenes from the movie *Prairie Justice* (Universal, 1938). In the first photo (above) you can see Bob Baker, his clothing and face. In the second photo (opposite) you can see Bob (?) making a transfer from his horse to the wagon. Is it Bob or a stuntman? The clothing is the same but you cannot see his belt in the transfer scene. The nose looks the same but the chin looks different in the second photo. Could be the angle. That's Carleton Young in the wagon, ready for the upcoming fight. The slot in the front of the wagon is where the reins go and a person lying on the floor of the wagon could drive the "runaway" wagon.

Bob Steele was one of the more prolific Western movie makers so let's look at one of his movies. In our picture we see Bob holding up the stagecoach as Jack Rockwell hands over the saddlebags. This scene is from *Brand of the Outlaws* (Supreme, 1936).

What we are looking for is to the right of Bob in the background. How could anyone miss that camera above the horse's neck? Just to the left of the camera are two people seated. The one on the left with a hat, holding something on his lap, could be the script supervisor. The man next to him with the long-sleeve white shirt could be the director. If it is the director, then that would be Robert M. Bradbury, Bob's father in real life.

This picture is from *No Man's Range* (Supreme,1935). This picture was directed by Bob Steele's father, Robert N. Bradbury. Bob is doing what he did in all of his films — fighting. As Bob sends the villain on his way, notice that the stunt man is looking to see where he will land. No need to worry. Look under the table and you will see a mattress and padding for him to land on.

Did You Notice?

The lead actor in this movie is Bob Allen (center) with the beautiful Eleanor Stewart on the right (what a long eyebrow). The man on the left is Jay Wilsey, also known as Buffalo Bill Jr. A star in silent and sound movies, he played more starring roles than Bob Allen did but was playing a supporting role when this movie, *The Rangers Step In* (Columbia, 1937), was filmed.

Looks like Bob is getting his Ranger star back from Jay, and Eleanor is not upset at all. Did you notice Bob's shirt collar, or lack of a collar? His shirt collar looks like one of the Nehru shirt collars that came out some years ago, but the photo is from 1937. Usually Bob wore a neckerchief and the missing collar was not so obvious as it is in this photo.

The wagon train is on its way west in Columbia's *Prairie Schooners* (1940). Star Bill Elliott is riding on the left of the wagon along with Evelyn Young. Sometimes the women would not wear a hat in outdoor scenes except in chase scenes where a stunt person would take over the part. Wearing a hat and the same clothes, viewers could not tell who it was.

Elliott's sidekick Dub Taylor is driving the wagon. You may remember him in the Frank Capra movie *You Can't Take It with You* (Columbia, 1938). A two-horse team was a little unusual for a prairie schooner. It could be that someone cut the budget. A guy on the far right is running to get out of the picture but he did not quite make it. No big rock or tree to hide behind.

This scene is from one of Tom Tyler's Monogram films, *Vanishing Men* (1932). The girl is Adele Lacy. I don't recall seeing Tom with crossed gun belts before but he's holding off the bad guys and protecting the girl. It's hard to identify any of the villains but I would bet that the guy in the middle is Charlie King. How about the door facings on each side at the top: horseshoes. The one on the left must have been for a pony. The horseshoes should point up for good luck. The thing I noticed was the carpet that awaits anyone going in or out of the house. Actually it's the corner of a larger carpet laid on the ground. This is one of the houses on the Walker Ranch; the Walker family lived in it at one time.

The Western Film Stills

In the photo this time there is nothing missing, nothing that should not be there, just two guys having a conversation. This picture is one that a lot of us (including myself) might look at and go on to something else. Then a little voice in our heads says, "Wait, go back." When you look again you discover that the guy on the left in western clothes is Humphrey Bogart and the dude in the double-breasted coat is western star George O'Brien. This scene is from *A Holy Terror* (Fox, 1931). It's called a B western by the "experts." It should be pointed out that the westerns made by O'Brian for Fox Studios were several notches above the average B western.

By the end of the movie, George is out of his suit and Bogart gets what the bad guys usually get. I don't know if Bogart ever acknowledged this film. Some big stars did not want to talk about or be reminded of their appearances in B westerns.

Did You Notice?

This first scene is from one of the movies that Johnny Mack Brown made for Universal Studios, *Arizona Cyclone* (1941). Johnny and Fuzzy Knight are in the covered wagon. Fuzzy was the sidekick at Universal for several western stars including Bob Baker, Johnny Mack Brown, Tex Ritter, Rod Cameron and Kirby Grant. The something that is out of place is behind the wagons and up on top of the rock formation. That's right, a utility pole with three crossbars.

The second photo (opposite) is on down the same road a little further; this photo is from one of the movies that Don "Red" Barry made at Republic Studios. Looks like Charlie King has the drop on Don Barry and his partner. Again you can see the pole and crossbars up on top of the rocks. Both scenes were taken at Corriganville.

The Western Film Stills

One of the essential elements of the Western movie was the fistfight. Some of the fights went on and on while in others only a few punches were thrown. These photos are from *Oklahoma Blues* (Monogram, 1948). In the first we see Jimmy Wakely delivering a right cross to some unlucky person. That blow even makes his hair stand up. In the background holding a rifle is Jimmy's sidekick Dub (Cannonball) Taylor. I don't think this kind of activity would help business at Joyce's Restaurant in the background.

Now let's look at the second photo (opposite). It looks like Jimmy has clobbered the same guy with a left cross this time. The guy's hair is still standing up. Dub is still holding the rifle with the unknown actor on the left and the restaurant lettering looks like it's in the Middle East. Actually what has happened is that when the second photo was printed, someone turned the negative over so that everything is reversed from what it was in the first photo.

The Western Film Stills

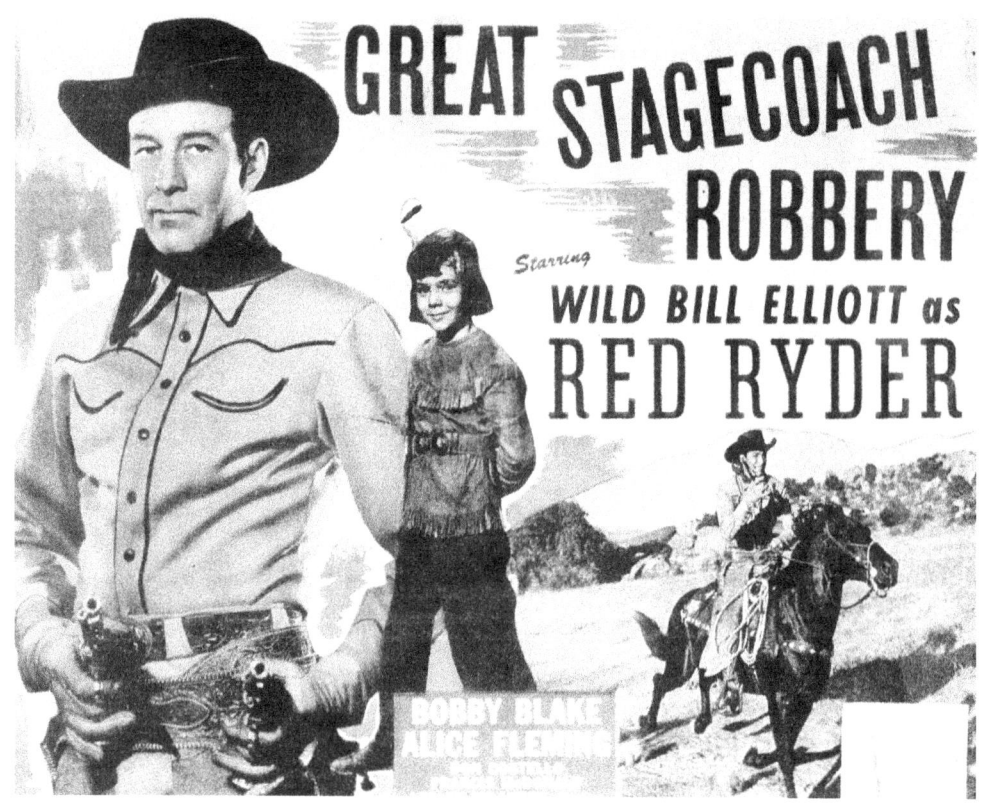

The Western Film Stills

The chase was another essential western element. Sometimes our heroes chased the lawbreaking members of society and other times it was the reverse. One thing for sure, it made an exciting time for the kids and I suspect for some of the adults in the back of the theater.

In the first picture is Bill Elliott from one of his Red Ryder movies chasing those outlaws. In the lower right hand corner you can see the shadows of the camera and some members of the filming crew. This would normally be the "Did you notice?" and I know that some of you are saying "I've seen that picture before," but wait.

To think that Republic would put out a photo like this to promote their movie is hard to believe. But they did make use of it. Look at the lobby card from *Great Stagecoach Robbery* (Republic, 1945) and you see the same picture in the lower right hand corner. Part of the shadows have been cut off and the Republic logo covers up most of the rest.

That's not the end of this picture. Now look at the lobby card of *Sheriff of Redwood Valley* (Republic, 1946). In the lower center we see the same picture of Wild Bill, only this time they did some trimming to cut out the shadows and the negative was turned over so now Bill is riding in the opposite direction and shooting left-handed.

These two movies were released within a year-and-a-half period. The thinking could have been that the kids would not notice or remember. Republic did make use of a photo that you usually don't see. Could have been economics.

Did You Notice?

These two pictures have something in common besides being from Western movies. In one photo Tom Tyler and his sidekick (actor unidentified) are looking at something in the distance and the something that I noticed is not the wire that was used to hold the chair together. In the other picture, Bob Livingston (third from left) and Guy D'Ennery are playing with a chair while Kenneth MacDonald holds onto Bob Steele. In the background, Yakima Canutt and Jack Ingram are ready to make sure the bad guys win this round. This scene is from a Three Mesquiteers movie, *Prairie Pioneers* (Republic, 1941).

The thing we are looking for is on the left side of the shirts of Tyler and Livingston. It looks like a giant centipede; actually it's a zipper. When these two were young and in their prime, they were broader across the shoulders than they were at the waist. This was also true of some of the other stars. The reverse was true for some in later years (and not just movie stars). When Tom and Bob wore a pullover shirt that was snug or form-fitting at the waist, then they put in a zipper on the side of the shirt, otherwise it would be difficult to get the shirt on and off.

Did You Notice?

This scene is from one of Bob Steele's films. It reminds me of the films he did for A.W. Hackel in the thirties. Bob, at right, is giving his "stink eye" look to the actor on the left who resembles Pat Brady, but this was before Pat's time in the movies. The oddball item in this still: No, it's not Jack Kirk, second from the right trying to look like one mean hombre, and it's not Ted Adams in the middle trying to keep the peace. It's the bus parked under the trees on the far left of the photo along with another vehicle.

    This photo is from the movie *Posse from Hell* (U-I, 1961) with John Saxon in the saddle. John has a gun belt but no belt for his pants and he is also using suspenders. This was an A-minus or B+ western so he could get by with that. Notice that he was wearing short boots as you can see his sock above the boot on the left side. The rocks in the background make the setting look like Lone Pine. The thing we are looking for: the tire marking from the camera car or, as Bud Thackery (cameraman at Republic Studios) would say, "the bucket of bolts."

How about a double feature from one movie. Back in 1932, Monogram made the movie *Hidden Valley*. In the first photo is our hero Bob Steele and our heroine Gertrude Messinger on the Goodyear Blimp. In the second photo you can see Gertrude and the pilot help Bob get into the passenger area of the blimp. The people in the lower right hand corner, holding on to a rope, are keeping things under control during the filming of this scene.

I wonder if Goodyear paid Monogram to have the blimp in the movie for exposure, or if Monogram paid Goodyear in order to have the blimp in the movie. It could have been a trade-off.

The Western Film Stills

Did You Notice?

How about a double feature where the photographer caught people in midair? The first photo is from one of Don "Red" Barry's Republic movies, but the person you see is not Barry — it's his double though it doesn't seem to be David Sharpe who doubled for Barry in the Red Ryder serial. The second photo is from the Allan Lane movie *Rustlers on Horseback* (Republic, 1950). Again, it's not Allan Lane doing what could become a dangerous stunt, but his double Tom Steele.

Look at the horses in each photo: Their eyes are covered by what looks like goggles. This keeps the horse from being distracted and moving around, and you sure don't want that to happen when you are on the way down.

Did You Notice?

This scene is from RKO's *Gunplay* (1951) with Tim Holt, Joan Dixon and Richard Martin. It was shot at the Jauregui Ranch. You can tell by the picket fence and the barn and corral in the background. The thing that is unusual in this picture is that guy in the background on the left behind the tree. That part of the picture is not in focus, but you can see the light reflecting off of his forehead. Most likely a member of the crew who forgot to duck.

The Western Film Stills

A scene from one of Charles Starrett's Columbia movies. The Sons of the Pioneers are providing the music for this party and Charlie is giving a tin cup of punch(?) to the well-rounded lady. The thing that I noticed in this B western is the number of people in this scene (41). The refreshments look like the real thing. I wonder if everyone got cake and cookies when the scene was finished. The Pioneers used their hats to decorate the wall behind them. How about the lights and lanterns (18)? They have corn stalks on the right and on both sides of the stage and jack-o'-lanterns at the top and to the right. I don't think they did much for Halloween in the time period of the Western movies.

Did You Notice?

This scene is from *Outlaw Express* (Universal, 1938) with Bob Baker and Cecelia Callejo. The two have posed for this picture, which was taken at the Monogram Ranch, renamed Melody Ranch when Gene Autry bought the property. This part of the ranch was not destroyed by the fire in 1962. This set was used as a fort, trading post, mission and hacienda as it was in this movie. The wooden floor on which the two leads are standing was used for some Spanish dancing during the movie.

The girl in the upper right hand corner is doing something to the set. She is not in the movie and the photographer caught her in the act.

The Western Film Stills

This scene is from Tex Fletcher's one and only full-length western, *Six Gun Rhythm* (1939). This film was made by Grand National, a company that did not last much longer than Fletcher's movie career. Tex was a lefty; you can see him in the center of the photo holding the coat of Reed Howes, who is sporting a mustache. To the left of Howes is Ted Adams looking at Fletcher as if to say, "You're not going to be around here very long."

Did you notice the extras? Some of the men and all of the women are dressed in the style of that time (1939). Perhaps the studio was trying to save money and not have everyone in western-style clothing. Now look in the lower right hand corner. What is all that stuff on the floor? Rope? Cable? It's extension cords for the lamps on each of the tables. No national safety regulations in those days.

Did You Notice?

    This is a scene taken with the camera level on top of the hitching rack on the left. At this level you don't see the electrical wires that were on all four sides of the Columbia Ranch in Burbank. This picture is from one of Charles Starrett's movies.

    Apparently Starrett or more likely his double has just transferred from his horse to the stagecoach which looks like a runaway (there's no driver in sight). Starrett lost his gun or he made the transfer with one hand while holding his gun on someone in the stagecoach. The "Did you notice?" in this photo is not something that should not be there, it's something that should be there — people. Other than Starrett (or his double) there are no people seen on this main street scene, only horses — eighteen.

Jimmy Wakely made a series of Western movies at Monogram from 1944 to 1949. This scene looks like it was shot at the Walker Ranch. The clue is the sycamore trees (white bark) in the background. Jimmy has just laid one on an unidentified actor and he did not even have his gloves on. Looks like he did not work up much of a sweat, but the villain will at least have a soft place to fall. Did you notice the two cars parked under the trees on the far left? The station wagon would be a collector's item today. I think Jimmy usually drove a Cadillac.

Did You Notice?

This scene is from the Three Mesquiteers *The Purple Vigilantes* (Republic, 1938). Bob Livingston is surrounded by the Purple Vigilantes and the head of the vigilantes Robert Fiske is holding a gun on him. Co-stars Ray Corrigan and Max Terhune are among the men on top of the large rocks in the background.

I don't think anyone would overlook the most interesting part of this still: the boom with the mike on it in the upper left hand corner. This scene looks like it was filmed at the Iverson Ranch. I wonder if the vigilantes costumes were really purple.

This photograph is from RKO's *Sunset Pass* (1946) with James Warren and Nan Leslie. I have no idea who the third person in the picture is, and when I talked to Jim Warren he did not know either, other than being "one of the crew." Jim said, "That photograph was taken at Lone Pine where we did the exteriors for this movie. The still photographer took pictures when we were not filming. A lot of times you would see photographs at the theater advertising a film but you would not see that exact same scene in the movie."

After viewing *Sunset Pass* I can say that this scene does not appear in the movie. There is a scene that is very similar to the photograph but the truck and third person are not present. If you have not found what should not be there, then look in the bottom right corner where you will see the rear end of a van with the door open and the third person facing the photographer.

A scene from the film *Nevada* (RKO, 1944) with Robert Mitchum. You can tell that the money the gambler is holding is not the real thing. This movie had a future Academy Award winner in the cast. This person is not listed in the credits and did not have any dialogue and is hard to pick out in the movie. But he was there. Look in the upper left hand corner; in the back you will see a young Ben Johnson, standing second from the left.

The Western Film Stills

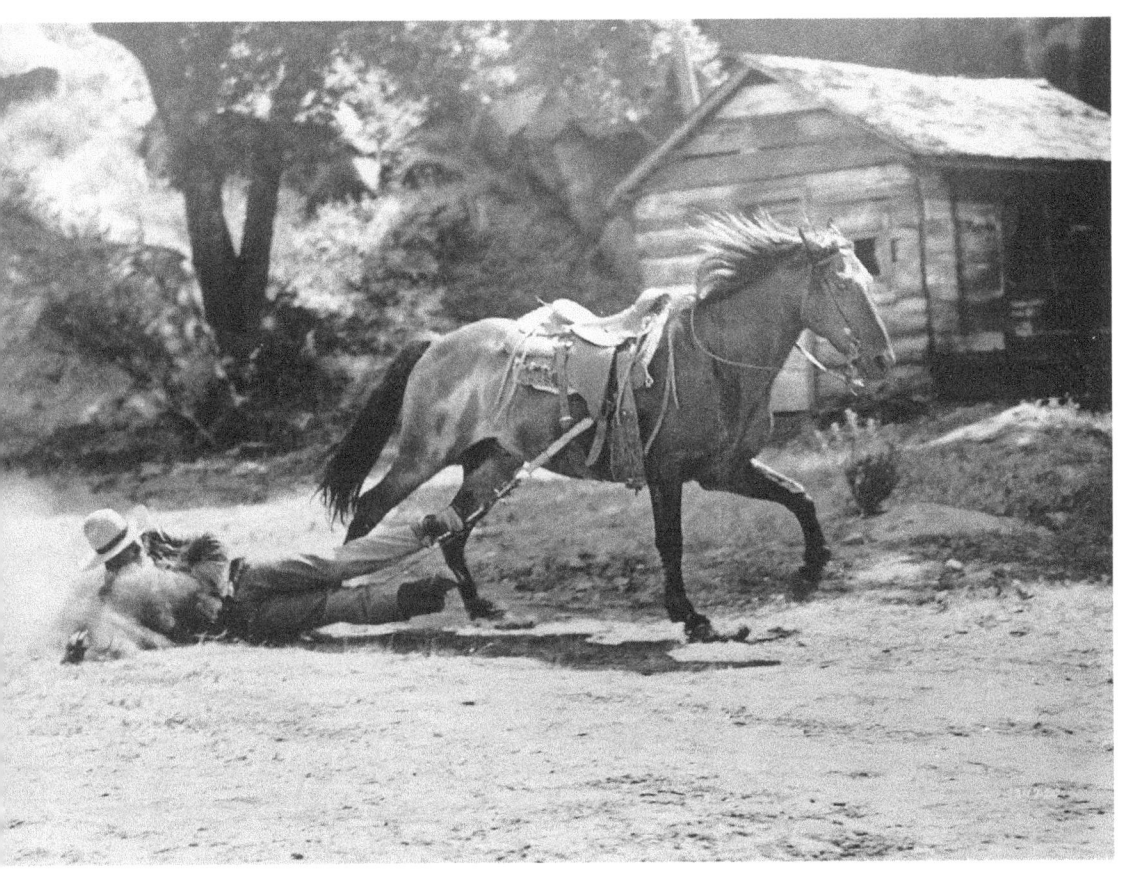

    This photo is from the movie *Deep in the Heart of Texas* (Universal, 1942), which starred Johnny Mack Brown and Tex Ritter. This scene does not appear in my tape of this film. A lot of movies have been cut and scenes that were in the original film are not in the copies we have today (thanks to TV time requirements). Also the costume of this person does not match with what the stars wore in this movie, except that Tex Ritter wore a white hat.

    This scene is called a saddle drag and usually in the movie you see it from a distance and it's over before you can notice any details. As you can see, the rider's foot is not caught in a regular stirrup — and did you notice that if the rider fell off the horse on the right side, then his right foot should be in the stirrup? Instead it's his left foot that is in the stirrup and his right foot is turned up so it does not get caught on anything on the ground. You can see that the foot is attached to a elongated device that allows the person being dragged to stay further away from the horse. The person being dragged has a trip that will release him from the horse when he pulls it. Also note that there is no saddle horn. When you're falling off a horse (on purpose) you don't want anything that could cause problems for you. Ouch!

Did You Notice?

One of *the* favorite western film heroes was Hopalong Cassidy, played by William Boyd. These two pictures are from the movie *Three Men from Texas* (Paramount, 1940). In the first picture (above), villain Dick Curtis is in the window opening and Hoppy has his gun hand on his knee trying to force the gun from Curtis' grasp. It seems that Curtis shows much more emotion than our hero, but then maybe that's the way it's supposed to be.

In the second picture (opposite), Hoppy has pulled Curtis through the window, the gun goes flying, Hoppy's hat covers his face, and — wait a minute. Curtis now has his hat on but in the first picture he did not have a hat on at all! How could Curtis have found his hat and put it on while in the steel grip of Hopalong Cassidy?

The Western Film Stills

These two pictures are from *Fort Osage* (Monogram, 1952) and the pictures were taken at the Monogram–Melody Ranch western street set. The girl driving the wagon is Jane Nigh; Rod Cameron is on the side of the wagon getting ready to step to the front of the wagon and take a seat beside Jane. It's obvious there was some kind of support for Rod to stand on.

The person in the other photo seems to be having trouble making the transfer: It's Rod's double and I don't think his legs were as long as Rod's. He is wearing the same clothing and riding the same horse (note the markings on the horse's head). After watching this movie I can tell you that Rod Cameron does the transfer himself. It seems a little odd that the photo with the double would be used to advertise the movie.

One thing I could not figure out was explained to me by a stuntman. In each picture the reins go from the horse to the rider. In each picture you will see another rein from the horse to the wagon. The stuntman said this was to keep the horse from straying away from the wagon during the transfer. This transfer was made at a slow speed. In the photo with Rod Cameron, where is the water barrel that was on the side of the wagon with the double? Actually I think it's a different wagon in each photo. In the photo with Rod you can see in the opening behind Jane what appears to be a rope at an angle, but this is not in the photo with Rod's double. Also the metal rod under Jane's boots is different in the two pictures. Did you notice the wagon seat in the two pictures? To the right of Jane the seat has a side piece connected to the back of the seat. On the other end of the seat — nothing. Makes it easier for the transfer.

Did You Notice?

These pictures are from Universal's "million dollar serial" *Riders of Death Valley* (1941) with Dick Foran, Buck Jones and a bunch of other people. I doubt if the million dollar tag referred to the salary of the people in the serial.

In one photo (opposite) we have four people in an action scene on horseback. In the other photo (above) we have (left to right) Buck Jones, Noah Beery, Jr., Dick Foran, "Big Boy" Williams and Leo Carrillo posing for a still shot.

Now try to match them up. In the action scene on the white horse, is it Buck Jones or is it a stuntman? It does not look much like Buck, but the costume does match. On the left is Leo Carrillo, or is it? He looks too big and slim for Leo. The guy in the back is Noah Beery Jr.? I don't think so. The person on the right should be Dick Foran. This still was filmed at Red Rock Canyon.

I think they are all stunt people doubling for the stars. Remember, when watching this movie the scenes go by very fast and there are so many things to see. But this time we did see the differences. Or did we?

The Western Film Stills

The Western Film Stills

Have you ever noticed the expressions on people's faces in a group shot? This picture of people on horseback is from *Under Arizona Skies* (Monogram, 1946). Johnny Mack Brown is in the lead and it looks like he's whistling or trying to. Ted Mapes on the right is riding with his eyes closed. He must trust his horse. Behind him is Riley Hill — serious. To the left is Reno Blair, squinting, and behind her is Kermit Maynard, who does not like the dust. On the far left is Raymond Hatton — just another day's work. Everyone uses two hands with their horse except Reno and Raymond — a woman and the oldest.

The second picture is from *Wild Horse Stampede* (Monogram, 1943). This was the first movie in the Trail Blazers series with Ken Maynard and Hoot Gibson. Maynard on the left has the drop on ten bad guys and has a serious expression. In the only film in this series where he wore a gun belt, Hoot, in the center, has a concerned expression while helping Bob Baker. The Oscar goes to Ian Keith on the right in front, who looks mad. Behind him is Ton London, and behind Tom is a guy with a smirk on his face and behind him up higher where all can see him is a guy smiling! Behind Hoot and Bob is Reed Howes, runner-up to Keith in the mad department. The guy just behind Maynard seems to have a fixation on Ken's guns. The expressions run the gamut in this picture. Oh, did you notice that Ian Keith is wearing a wedding band on his left hand? I did not know that the bad guys were ever married in the B Western movies.

Two easy goofs this time. The first picture is from the Texas Rangers series' *The Whispering Skull* (PRC, 1944) with Dave O'Brien and Denny Burke. I did not recognize the girl in the picture and in looking up the cast the only female part listed was credited to Denny Burke.

The second photo is of Bob Baker and his pinto horse. There was no picture credit with the photo; it could be just a publicity shot. It's a nice picture except we could do without the car in the background on the far right. Bob made most of his movies in the late thirties and the windows in the car look small but that's the way they were made at that time. In the Texas Rangers photo, again on the right, in the background is car. The Rangers films were made in the mid-forties and the car looks to be pre–World War II as no cars were made during the war. I think in both pictures the still photographer just made a mistake; no cars were intended to be in the picture.

The Western Film Stills

Did You Notice?

This scene is from the first western that Republic Pictures made, *Westward Ho* (1935). Did you notice the young cowboy in the center, strumming the guitar? Why, it's Marion Michael Morrison, aka John Wayne. In the movie Wayne is not in this scene. The person behind Wayne plays the guitar and Wayne is off to the side cogitating.

To the left of Wayne is Jack Kirk. On the far right is Glenn Strange who is remembered by the TV generation as Sam the bartender on *Gunsmoke*. In the movie Wayne does serenade Shila Mannors, the female lead, and it sounds like Jack Kirk. Others say that Bob Steele's brother William Bradbury did the singing for Wayne.

In this photo you should have noticed that all of the horse are white, all 19 of them. But did you notice that all of the men are wearing white neckerchiefs? All 18 of them, some singing, some listening, some stretched out taking a nap (and two are up in the rocks of Lone Pine). This group, The Singing Riders, rode white horses and wore white neckerchiefs so they would not shoot each other when they fought the outlaw gang that rode dark horses and wore black (or no) neckerchiefs.

The Western Film Stills

It looks like Tex Ritter has the situation well in hand because George Pembroke is having second thoughts about drawing his gun. If he does draw, you know he's a goner and the movie is almost over. That coat that Pembroke is wearing looks out of place even with the king size elbow patches. On the left is Carleton Young and the henchman next to Tex is Wally West, who starred in some silent westerns. Did you notice that Bob Steele was also in this photo? You can see him just above Wally's shoulder on the bulletin board: WANTED FOR MURDER. Bob made some movies about the same time as this movie was made so I think we can assume that the wanted poster was left over from one of Bob's pictures. The girl is Pauline Haddon. This scene is from *Cowboy from Sundown* (Monogram, 1940) and was filmed at the Monogram Ranch.

The first time I saw at this photo from an unidentified movie, I looked at it again and again. I'm still not sure what is going on. Sometimes that was not unusual in a PRC film, which I think this is.

Al "Fuzzy" St. John, who was the sidekick to more cowboys then we have room to list, is holding back Charlie King. Charlie has a badge sticking out of his pocket which is an oddity because Charlie was usually the villain. Of course he could have been a crooked sheriff in the film. Now Fuzzy and Charlie have their guns on someone but the guys behind them have their hands up. Is that guy on the left going to get the drop on Fuzzy and Charlie so these reprobates can get away or is he helping Fuzzy and Charlie by keeping his gun on all of these bad guys? If he tried to shoot one of the men on the right side, he would have to shoot through the post, Fuzzy and Charlie. Give up? The guy on the far right with his face hidden also has a gun on these men. You can see part of the gun under the arm of the guy on the right with the baggy pants. I first thought this same person had bandages on the palms of both of his hands but a second look shows me that it just happened that the sun shining through this collection of bodies just happened to shine on the same part of each hand.

The Western Film Stills

In this scene from *Old Overland Trail* (Republic, 1953), Rex Allen and Slim Pickens ride on down the trail. Look at the background on the far right side of the picture. Looks like some kind of wooden structure built in the rocks with a door or window in it and some type of barbed wire fencing around it. The second thing that I noticed was that Slim's horse does not have a bit in its mouth, just a rope halter called a hackamore. While watching this movie I could not help but notice how much larger Rex's horse was in comparison to Slim's horse and also how much larger Slim was than Rex. This made me feel sorry for Slim's horse.

Did You Notice?

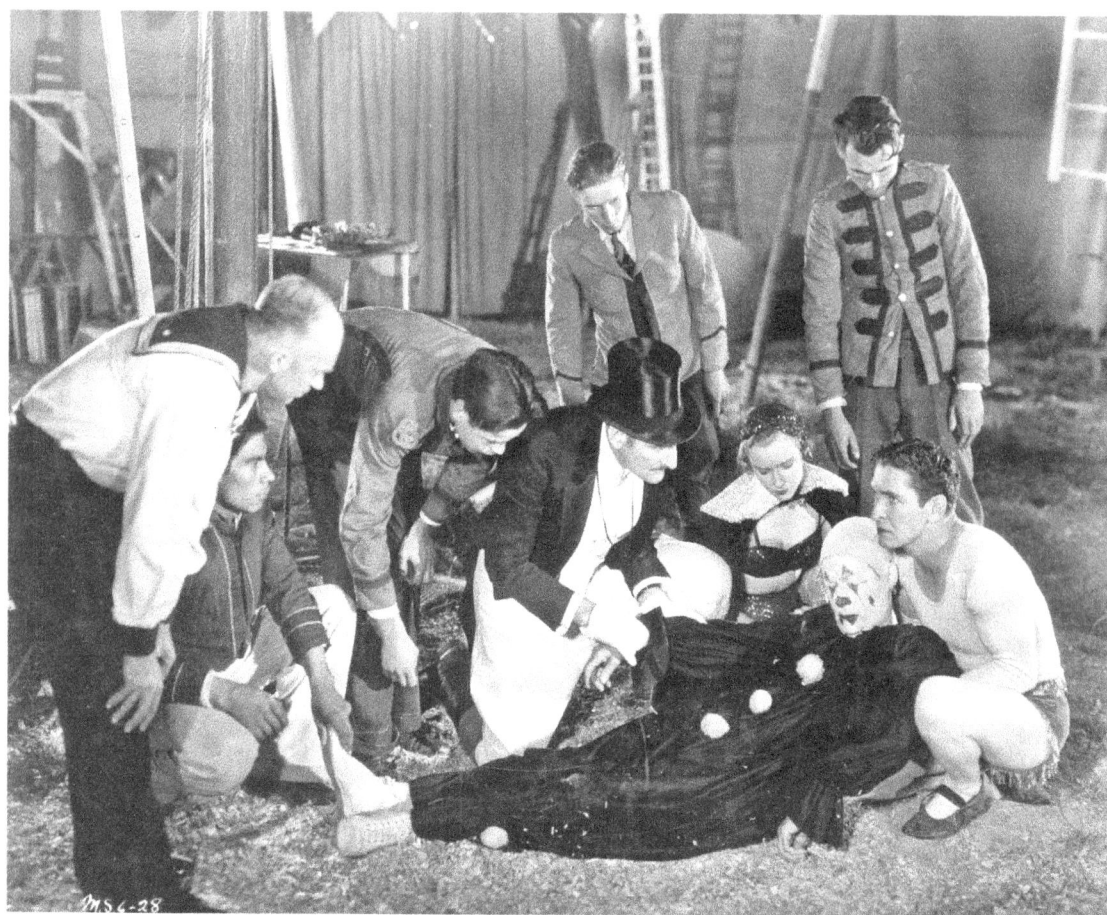

The film is *The Gallant Fool* (Monogram, 1933) starring Bob Steele. Theodore Lorch (in top hat), Arletta Duncan the heroine and our hero Bob Steele are gathered around the clown on the ground. The clown was played by our old friend George Hayes, before he became "Gabby." Bob is dressed in his costume as a high wire aerialist in the circus. This is a Western movie? Sort of. Take a look at the second photo. Perry Murdock and John Elliott (on the left) and other people that were in the first photo are now dressed like they belong in a Western movie. In this movie, more time is spent in the circus tent than out on the range or in the saloon. We must say that Bob had nerve. Could you see your favorite cowboy in that aerialist costume?

Did You Notice?

This scene is from *The Pinto Bandit* (PRC, 1944), one of the films in the Texas Rangers series. There were three Rangers in this film but in this picture we have only one, Dave "Tex" O'Brien in the center. Looks like Dave is about to get a knot on his head from Jack Ingram on the right. Jack was the brains of the outlaw gang, got to wear the suit, vest, white shirt, and tie. Dave can't go very far to his right because one of the all-time great villains Charles King has his gun on him. The way Charlie is dressed, you know he is not the leader of the outlaw gang. The only way out of this for Dave is to slip off of his horse and run to the right and borrow one of the two cars. Just be careful that he does not trip over the reflector lying on the ground.

The Western Film Stills

In Westerns, the shootout or gunfight was a common occurrence. In *Rustlers Roundup* (Universal, 1946), one of the combatants (actor unidentified) has just taken a slug and holds his hand over his shoulder wound. If you look closely you will see he has a wedding ring on that hand and that is a very unusual thing to see in a B western. The man next to the wounded man is Ethan Laidlaw, who most of the time was an outlaw. So these men could be the villains. Besides the wedding ring, did you notice the man on the far right in front of the next building reading his newspaper? He does not seem to be concerned about the gunfight.

Did You Notice?

This time we have scenes from two movies and the thing that we are looking for is rather obvious in each photo. One scene is from *Heart of the Rio Grande* (Republic, 1942) and it looks like Gene Autry and Fay McKenzie are leading a group of cowboys and cowgirls on a little ride. Joe Strauch (Tadpole) is trying to get his horse into place, Jean Porter is lined up behind Gene and in the back of the group is Smiley Burnette, whose face is partly hidden by the hat of Edith Fellows. To the right of Edith is Pierre Watkin. The rest of the gang wait their turn to get in the procession.

The other scene has Bill Elliott being held at gunpoint by Betty Miles from the movie *The Return of Daniel Boone* (Columbia, 1941). It must be early in the movie as Bill was usually on the same side as the girl.

"Shadows" could be a subtitle for this story as that is what we notice in each photo. In the Autry photo you can see in the lower left hand part of the picture the mike boom, the operator and several other items. In the Elliott photo on the left side you can again see a shadow, I assume a mike boom. One other thing I noticed in the Autry photo: Gene and Fay have their smiles on for the camera; the rest will have their smiles on by the time they come within camera range.

The Western Film Stills

Did You Notice?

In this picture from an unknown film we have the stagecoach coming down the road in a hurry. We know that someone is chasing the coach because if you look at the last window on the coach you can see a gun sticking out, ready to fire at someone. At the door you can see a hand and someone in a white hat. Could it be our hero?

The other people in the picture don't seem to be concerned about the situation. Look in the background between the two teams of horses pulling the coach. There is a saddled white horse. On the other side of the tree you can see someone with a light-colored shirt and hat.

The Western Film Stills

A photo from *Border Wolves* (Universal, 1938) with Bob Baker seated on the upturned wash tub and his sidekick Fuzzy Knight to Bob's right. I don't recognize the other members of the gang. They all seem to be concerned about something in the distance. The guy behind Fuzzy has committed a no-no: He's looking directly into the camera which violates one of the basic rules of movie making.

Did You Notice?

The subject for these two photos could be how to tie up or not to tie up those palefaces. The first photo is from the serial *Wild West Days* (Universal, 1937) with Johnny Mack Brown and Lynn Gilbert. This method of tying the hands is tiring and limits the movement of the individual, but the two captives don't seem to be overly concerned. Look at the way Lynn is tied. The rope around the wrists is all right, the rope is tied on the back of the tree and you can see the loop of the rope on each side of the tree and the end of the rope on each side. It would not take much effort to grab one end of the rope and pull. The knot on Johnny's hands does not look very difficult either. In the background is Iron Eyes Cody in the center.

The Western Film Stills

The second photo is from the serial *Overland with Kit Carson* (Columbia, 1939) with Bill Elliott, Iris Meredith, an Indian and Pegleg the mysterious villain in the background on the right. Bill does not seem to be worried at all but Iris seems a little concerned. You will notice that Bill's hands are not tied so he could reach up with his left hand and grab the Indian. He could also pull the Indian closer and use his knee — whoops, scratch that — they did not do that in those days. Anyway, you have two methods of being tied up or not to be tied up. Maybe the Indians in each movie were from different tribes.

Did You Notice?

Stagecoaches were seen in many Western movies. We never had much time to look at the stagecoach up close as the stage was usually moving on along the trail trying to keep up with the music.

Our scene here is from *Take Me Back to Oklahoma* (Monogram, 1940), as Tex Ritter in the driver's seat sneaks a peek at his passenger Terry Walker . Look at the part of the stagecoach just below the sign that says U.S. MAIL. This beautifully carved leather piece had to be custom-made and no doubt the piece on the other side is the same. In the lobby card this part is brown but it's possible that it could be made of metal and painted brown. Either way, it's a nice-looking addition to the stagecoach.

The Western Film Stills

The stagecoach is being held up by the outlaws and they are taking the strongbox. This is from *Gun Smoke* (Monogram, 1945). The man taking the strongbox looks like Marshall Reed and he *was* in this movie. Notice the guy on the far left, the wrangler who is more interested in taking care of the horses than the stagecoach holdup.

Did You Notice?

This scene is from *North of the Border* (Screen Guild, 1945). The two adversaries are Russell Hayden on the right and Douglas Fowley on the left. Fowley must be the "brains" of the outlaw gang. In the B westerns the brains heavy was usually a lawyer, a banker or a politician and they wore a coat. Notice on the right side of the photo a wrangler who did not get out of the picture; he is more interested in the horse than the troubles of Hayden and Fowley.

The Western Film Stills

The movie ads in the newspapers and lobby cards at the theater were very important to the youngsters of long ago. The scenes displayed of the coming movies would help you decide which movie house to go to the following week, unless there was only one theater in town. Most theaters would have a display of coming movies which would entice people back.

For some reason the people who made up the ads and pictures of Johnny Mack Brown could not decide if Johnny was left handed or right handed. Actually what happened was that the person making up the ads and pictures inadvertently turned the negative over and Johnny became a left-handed cowboy several times.

In this lobby card from *Colorado Ambush* (Monogram, 1951) you can see Johnny as a right-handed *and* left-handed gunman. In the center, Johnny has his gun in his right hand and is ready for trouble. Look at the scene in the lower left hand corner and you will see that Johnny has his gun on his left side. If they had used *un-*flipped, Johnny would cover up the front part of the horse. So just flip the negative and most of the shot of Johnny riding the horse can be seen.

Cinemart Productions presents "TRIGGER PALS" with ART JARRETT, LEE ("Lone Ranger") POWELL, AL ST. JOHN. A Phil Krasne Production - A Grand National Release

The Western Film Stills

These two pictures are from the movie *Trigger Pals* (Grand National, 1939) with (in the first photo) Art Jarrett, Lee Powell and Al St. John. Art Jarrett was a vocalist with various bands including Ted Weems and took over the Hal Kemp Band in 1941 after Kemp was killed in an auto crash.

Lee Powell had the lead in two 1938 Republic serials, *The Lone Ranger* and *The Fighting Devil Dogs*. After *Trigger Pals*, Lee made a series of westerns at PRC with Art Davis and Bill Boyd (not Hoppy). In 1942 he joined the U.S. Marines and saw action in the Pacific during World War II.

Al St. John, the third member of this trio, had been around from the days of the silent movies, when he was one of Mack Sennett's Keystone Cops. St John developed the character of Fuzzy Q. Jones while working in a series of pictures with Fred Scott, and Fuzzy or St. John just went on and on.

When Lee Powell left Republic, he went on tour with the Wallace Bros. Circus and was billed as the "Lone Ranger" as he had played that part in the *Lone Ranger* serial. The rights owners of the "Lone Ranger" brought court action to restrain Lee from using the title of the Lone Ranger. It's been reported that Lee won in the first court case but in appeals the judgment came in favor of the corporation. *Trigger Pals* was released in 1939 so it was in circulation before the court order took effect, and you'll see that "Lone Ranger" has been crossed out at the bottom of the photo. A lot of films were re-released several times during the war years (1941–1945) and all that was necessary to comply with the court order was a little ink. In the lobby card you can see the original billing.

Did You Notice?

Lash LaRue has just given it to some unfortunate person. You can tell it's Lash as he has his name on his belt in front. This action is from *Vanishing Outpost* (Western Adventure, 1951).

At first I thought that Lash had hit a woman. With that long hair flying around and the front of the shirt ... protruding. But my sense's returned and I knew that Lash would not hit a woman. Just to make sure, I dug out this movie on tape. It was just one of the guys who needed a haircut, wearing a loose shirt.

In the second photo Lash has just served Jack Ingram a knuckle sandwich in *Son of a Badman* (Western Adventures-Screen Guild, 1949). In the second the photographer got both Lash and Jack from the front. Makes it easier to identify them.

Did You Notice?

A friendly game of cards was a common occurrence in westerns. Usually the game did not end up with everyone satisfied. In our scene Bill Elliott in the Red Ryder film *Marshal of Reno* (Republic, 1944) is showing his cards to one of the other players with a little smirk that says "you should know better than to cheat me." The player on the right is Marshall Reed. Some of the onlookers around the table look familiar from watching them over the years.

There are three things that I noticed in this picture. The guy on the far right leaning on the bar with his back to the camera is not wearing a western outfit. I wonder if he was part of the crew and did not realize that he was in this shot. The second thing is the bottle on the table with the cap on. The bottle will be used later in a fight. If you used the bottle to hit someone without the top on, then the contents would be all over you. Finally, did you ever see anyone play cards with their gloves on like Bill Elliott?

The key word in this picture could be condition. Our hero Reb Russell in the center made nine movies for Kent in 1934 and '35. He is outnumbered in this situation. What is the guy on the right so happy about? He's the only one who does not have his gun out. I'd get off of that porch before it falls down. Look at the wall of the cabin. Looks like logs, but it's not, just boards with bark (fake or real) attached to the board. Between the boards is supposed to be caulking (filler). Look behind the man close to Reb. You can see what looks like a thin board between the log boards. Now look up above Reb and the girl and you can see where someone tried to patch up the caulking and some of it is coming out. I noticed that all the men have clean, well-blocked hats and the guy on the left has a lot of rivets in his holster and belt.

Did You Notice?

One of the all time Western favorites Gene Autry (center) waves with June Storey on the right and Mary Lee on the left. Gene, June, Mary and all of the people in the photo are saying what I am saying with this installment: not goodbye, just so long for awhile. Perhaps I'll come back with more of this type of material some time. I hope you got a laugh now and then. Thanks to those who helped identify films and people in the pictures.

Oh! I almost forgot. Did you notice the person in the upper left hand corner of the photo? The guy with the pipe in his mouth? What in the world is he doing up there? Maybe he just wanted to say "So long!" with the rest of the gang. Until next time, "Did You Notice?"

Index

Abbott and Costello 135
Adams, Ted 34, 154
Allen, Bob 36, 40, 81, 84, 142
Andrews, Slim 56
Atchley, Hooper 32
Ates, Roscoe 56
Autry, Gene 58, 76, 114, 119, 188, 204

Baker, Bob 20, 21, 30, 50, 57, 62, 66, 82, 97, 106, 117, 135, 137–139, 162, 179, 191
Bannon, Jim 85
Barkley, Don 13
Barrett, Curt and the Trailsmen 72
Barry, "Red" Don 127, 147, 158
Beebe, Marjorie 22
Bell, Rex 78
Bennett, Ray 85
Berry, Noah, Jr. 174, 175
Blair, Reno 177
Blake, Pamela 12
Bogart, Humphrey 145
Bond, Ward 102, 121
Booth, Adrian *see* Gray, Lorna
Boyd, William 11, 170, 171
Brent, Roy 129
Brown, Johnny Mack 14, 26, 28, 57, 63, 104, 117, 118, 123, 128, 130, 131, 136, 142, 197
Brown, Reno 86
Buffalo Bill, Jr. 17, 126, 142
Burke, Denny 178
Burr, Raymond 112
Buster, Budd 80

Calvet, Corinne 131
Cameron, Rod 172
Cansino, Rita 107
Canut, Yakima 9, 71, 83, 153
Carrillo, Leo 93, 174, 175
Carson, Sunset 39
Chandler, Lane 71, 100
Chesebro, George 95
Clyde, Andy 11, 86, 87
Coates, Phyllis 12
Corbet, Ben 31, 71

Corrigan, Ray 28, 58, 98, 107, 116, 166
Crabbe, Buster 8, 124
Curtis, Dick 118, 170, 171

Davis, Art 38
D'Ennery, Guy 153
Dixon, Joan 160
Duncan, Arletta 184
Dwire, Earl 80

Elliott, Bill 12, 24, 38, 46, 61, 110, 143, 150, 151, 188, 192, 202
Elliott, John 33, 77
Ellis, Frank 16, 121

Farnum, Franklyn 9, 38
Farrell, Tommy 86
Ferguson, Al 38
Fiske, Robert 166
Fitzgerald, Ella 135
Fleming, Susan 10
Fletcher, Tex 163
Foran, Dick 174, 175
Forman, Carol 113
Fowley, Douglas 196

Gail, Robert 108
Gibson, Hoot 80, 176
Gilbert, Lynn 192
Gilbert, Nina 80
Gould, William 66, 108, 109
Grant, Kirby 28, 29, 48, 49, 129
Gray, Lorna 28

Hackett, Karl 192
Haddon, Pauline 181
Hall, Lois 197
Hart, John 12
Hatton, Raymond 88, 119, 196
Hayden, Russell 88, 119, 196
Hayes, George 184, 185
Healey, Myron 13
Holt, Jennifer 26, 136
Holt, Tim 96, 101, 104, 117, 118, 123, 128
Howard, Ed 129
Howes, Reed 176

Ingram, Jack 14, 23, 153, 186
Isley, Phyllis 176

January, Lois 44
Jarrett, Art 198
Jenks, Si 52
Johnson, Ben 168
Jolley, I. Stanford 53, 95
Jones, Buck 10, 15, 41, 120, 121, 174, 175

Keene, Tom 35, 128
Keith, Ian 176
King, Charles 38, 144, 182, 186
King, John 69
Kirby, Jay 11
Kirk, Jack 21, 154, 180
Knight, Fuzzy 26, 29, 117, 123, 146, 191
Kohler, Fred 15
Kortman, Bob 36, 84

Lacy, Adele 144
Laidlaw, Ethan 187
Lane, Allen 54, 159
Lane, Richard 135
Larie, Nora 32, 52
LaRue, Lash 200, 201
Lease, Rex 80, 132, 136
Leslie, Nan 167
Livingston, Bob 42, 50, 58, 107, 114, 118
Long, Audry 95
Lorch, Theodore 184, 185
Luden, Jack 37
Lyden, Jack 129

MacDonald, Kenneth 128, 152
Martin, Jill 33
Martin, Richard 160
Mathews, Carl 103
Maynard, Ken 70, 76, 176
Maynard, Kermit 16, 22, 124, 177
McCarthy, Patti 8
McCoy, Tim 32, 33, 34, 44, 52
McIntyre 14
McKenzie, Bob 28, 79
McKenzie, Fay 188

Index

McKim, Sam 28, 58, 113
Meredith, Iris 193
Merton, John 50
Messinger, Gertrude 156
Miles, Betty 188
Miller, Walter 36, 84
Mitchum, Bob 11, 168
Moreland, Mantan 68
Murdock, Perry 184
Murphy, Horace 118

Nelson, Horace 118
Nolan, Bob 18

Oakman, Wheeler 110
O'Brien, Dave 178, 196
O'Brien, George 102, 145
Osborne, Bud 16, 24, 32, 36, 38, 84

Palmer, Tex 16
Pembroke, George 181
Peters, House 74
Pickins, Slim 183
Porter, Jean 188
Powell, Lee 198
Powers, Richard *see* Keene, Tom

Reed, Marshall 63, 72, 195, 202
Renaldo, Duncan 90, 93

Rice, Frank 108, 109
Ritter, Tex 25, 26, 63, 64, 181, 194
Rockwell, Jack 82, 140
Roland, Gilbert 73
Russell, Reb 203

St. John, Al 105, 182, 198
Sawyer, Joe 32
Saxon, John 155
Saylor, Sid 53
Scott, Fred 92, 105
Sharpe, David 69, 105
Sons of the Pioneers 161
Starrett, Charles 18, 95, 122, 161, 164
Steele, Bob 30, 42, 46, 53, 140, 141, 153, 154, 156, 181, 184, 185
Steele, Karen 125
Stewart, Eleanor 142
Story, June 204
Strange, Glenn 56, 82, 180
Strauch, Joe (Tadpole) 188

Talbot, Lyle 110
Taliaferro, Hal 9, 37, 63, 78
Tamblyn, Russ 133
Taylor, Dub 143, 148, 149
Terhune, Max 28, 58, 69, 98, 99, 115, 116, 166

The Texas Rangers 196
Tibbetts, Martha 36, 84
Tyler, Tom 22, 60, 79, 101, 108, 109, 144, 154

Vale, Virginia 134

Wakely, Jimmy 148, 149, 165
Wales, Wally *see* Taliaferro, Hal
Waling, William 10
Walker, Terry 194
Waller, Eddy 113
Warren, James 95, 112, 167
Watkin, Pierre 188
Wayne, John 10, 29, 98, 99, 100
Weldon, Marion 42
Whitaker, Slim 66, 79, 108, 109, 132
White, Lee (Lasses) 96
Whitley, Ray 96
Wills, Chill 102
Wilson, Whip 86, 87
Windsor, Marie 46
Wisley, Jay *see* Buffalo Bill, Jr.
Woods, Harry 38
Worden, Hank 97

Young, Carleton 82, 138
Young, Evelyn 143
Young, Polly Ann 120

www.ingramcontent.com/pod-product-compliance
Ingram Content Group UK Ltd.
Pitfield, Milton Keynes, MK11 3LW, UK
UKHW050526150426
5217IPUK00026B/1820